THE LAST GOOD SNOW HUNT

JOSHUA DEWAIN FOSTER

Copyright © 2024 Joshua Dewain Foster

Published by Foster Literary

First Printing June 2024

Paperback: 979-8-9878191-1-1

Cover Art by Spencer Erickson, Son of Erik Design

All rights reserved.

Without limiting the rights under copyright reserved above, no part of this publication may be reproduced, stored in or introduced in a retrieval system, or transmitted, in any form, or by any means (electronic, mechanical, photocopying, recording, or otherwise), without the prior written permission of both the copyright owner and the above publisher of this book—except in the case of brief quotations embodied in critical articles and reviews.

To request information or permissions, contact the publishers at FosterLit.com

PUBLISHER'S NOTE:

This is a work of nonfiction. Even so, names, characters, places, and incidents either are the product of the author's imagination or are used fictitiously, and any resemblance to actual persons, living or dead, events, or locales is entirely coincidental—except when they are not.

Foster Literary

DEDICATION

To JBF,

my only son;

remember, oh remember—

safety first.

CONTENTS

1	THE GHOST ELK
6	YOUR MA AND YOU
13	YOUR GRANDPA
19	LUPINE LOU
26	ME
32	ANOTHER WEIRD YEAR
39	GO BAG
44	RENDEVOUS
51	ROAD HUNT
61	WHEN IN DOUBT
67	SUNRISE SHOVEL
71	SUCCEEDING TO FAIL
78	FAILING TO SUCCEED
88	CHARGE
93	STALK
101	SHOT
115	EXTRACTION
126	DECONSTRUCTION
136	DUES
142	YOU AGAIN
150	SUPPERTIME
	ACKNOWLEDGEMENTS

THE GHOST ELK

Your Grandpa taught me to keep my eyes open and my mouth shut, especially on the elk hunt. This proved impossible; sure, I could spy, but I couldn't ever stop myself from running my big fat bottom lip. All it took was one other person to get me asking questions, and I'd start yapping. That's just how I've always been.

When I was eleven, and your Grandpa and I were up in the Antelope Hills one fall afternoon, I wouldn't stop asking him about rocks or sagebrush or the tint of the sky or the best elk he'd ever seen. The word was out on a big herd of elk moving back and forth across the hills. We were hoping we'd catch them on our stretch of fence.

At the bottom of the mountain road, your Grandpa stopped the pickup and made me get out of the cab and into the pickup bed to scout from there. I sat on the wheel well with my .22, and your Grandpa got going up the hill on the lumber road. I scanned on one side the aspens, and on the other the pines. The air smelled wet, snow coming, we could all feel that, and I carried my little rifle for pine hens.

I was still too young to bring down big game. That did not stop me from acting like a true woodsman. I kept my green eyes peeled for sign. I had long read the westerns and scout manuals. I'd been trained in the shooting arts by your Grandpa, the farmers, neighbors, friends and relatives. This was the first big hunt for me, though, everyone else arriving soon, the two of us scouting alone.

The farm pickup banged on the big exposed rocks in the ragged logging road. The suspension creaked, the bed shifted, the trees swayed in a stiff breeze. The dry leaves wisped and whispered and crunched all around. Once or twice my gun clattered across the metal bed. As sneaky as a tank, maybe, or a gang of rhinos. To be honest, I wasn't sure what I was searching for. I just opened my eyes wide as I could and tried to spot through the dust.

I was doing just that when I saw what looked like a tree, walking. As the dirt curtain dissipated, and your Grandpa slowed down to creep through some tree overhang, I realized that the limbs I'd seen were two big antler branches, bigger than any I'd ever seen hung on a wall or in a garage.

Out onto the road behind us stepped a giant, stealthy bull, his head raised and all his points to the sky. The setting sun and drifting dust gave the beast an aura and a patina. As tall as a horse, but with spikes installed, heavy ones that would take a strong neck. The elk gleamed like the driven snow. An alabaster elk, a massive albino. All white.

    I made no sound. I couldn't. I was mesmerized by the glowing bull. I didn't even raise my gun, really didn't have time, wouldn't dare insult it. Quiet, elegant, dainty on its hooves; three long silent steps, and the great pale elk vanished.

    At the top of the hill, I banged on the window and told your Grandpa through the back slider window. He pulled me inside and sat me up and told me to tell him everything. So I started from sunrise that morning and noted all the details of the day and he tuned me out and retraced the road back down the hill, spying out the window. No sign. At the bottom, where we were all staying in the old hunting cabin, I told all the other hunters who had arrived about the ghost elk. They grew agitated and went through their gear and guns and stared out the porch window into the black night wondering about the white bull. Would they be the ones to get it? We all slept in one room in sleeping bags on the floor.

    We awoke long before sunrise to two feet of new snow. The world had changed overnight, and so had the hunt. We, for one, had just gotten much more deadly. This, whiteout, our people's only true camouflage state.

At daybreak, in one big group, ten or so of us went trudging on foot up and over the first hill where we encountered a giant herd of elk in the back pasture, bedded down in the mountain hay, lumps in snow. Maybe three-hundred elk out there, in a giant orbit. We spread out and spaced out and on a hand-signal, stood them up.

We bagged five very fine, very large bull elk, and two cow elk. I didn't shoot anything, but I was stuck with the processing crew on all seven animals, and for two days straight we took the elk apart with knives and saws and our own hands, until we'd stripped the beauties of all we could consume.

The ghost elk escaped. Was not seen that morning, never seen again. That made me feel better about things. I would have hated to gut it and splay it, loathed to make that ivory hide blood-spatted, gotten sad to see its big rack and head and no body leaving the hills for good, tied down with neon moto-straps on a farm flatbed.

My sighting of the ghost elk had been miraculous, a visitation. The gore that followed tempered my desire to take big game. I did not want to inflict myself upon the world like that. I did not want to minus the earth of such beauty just for my belly. I was not hungry enough yet to do that.

Then you showed up.

YOUR MA AND YOU

Genealogically, your Ma lived most of her life on the Gulf Coast of Alabama; Mobile Bay, to be exact, and the swamps and rivers and beaches surrounding it. She grew up reading books and exploring the woods and writing poems in her head. Crabbing off the pier and fishing along the creek. She also had a machete and muddy feet, rowed herself in a canoe a lot too. She would have had a dad out there teaching her a lot of things, but he died too young, tragically. Your southern Grandpa, Jenkins III, murdered at work, lost at sea.

Without Jenkins III, your Granny and your Great Grandpa Sandy took your Ma fishing, and they'd share hunting bounty of deer, turkey, shrimp, snapper. Your Ma, she grew a wild, wide, gamey palette, and was eternally jealous of her girl cousins with dads who could take them out in the woods to hunt. She never did agree much with being a girl. She wanted the whole spectrum of human experience, and mostly taught herself everything she ever wanted to know. Had to be that way, without a dad. Had to learn everything the hard way. She was even vegan for a spell, supposedly. For political and ethical reasons. In her more radical days. That's what happens.

By the time I met her, your Ma had learned to cook just about anything up, and had nerves and guts to snap and crack through any carcass. I loved her as soon as I knew that, knew we'd get along as soon as we started sharing meals. She taught me how to suck the head of a mudbug. We met in Texas, and our first date was over a crawfish boil on her birthday. First time I'd ever tried that, and it turned out to be something I'd always wanted but didn't know existed.

Hot, boiled, spicy potatoes—your Ma changed my life that first night, all in a sweat.

After we moved in together, when your Ma and I were schooling in Houston, long before you, we were four together with your two older siblings in a small flat divided with curtains, we ate cans of tuna fish and chicken, cheese on chips, noodles, red beans, occasionally went in with the upstairs neighbors to smoke a pork roast. Sundays I'd splurge and make everyone tacos with cheap Texas burger or stew meat. Maybe once a year we'd get lucky to scrape enough time and coin together to go out to a proper crawfish boil. We started buying boil ingredients in bulk, inviting over the neighbors and writers to share in the food.

By the time we finished our PhD's, we were skinny and hungry and full of want to stay together. Your Ma and I, unmarried but having found each other after all these years, were willing to do whatever we had to do to continue as a family unit. Your Grandpa hired us to move to Idaho and run a wedding venue he'd just purchased. Your Ma and I had four divorces between us—we knew all about weddings. We were ten-thousand-hour marriage experts. So we moved everything and everyone and all the pets to Idaho. In part, too, I wanted to be back home to help your Grandpa with his farm, as the church was sending him and your Grandma far away, to preside for three years in charge of a proselytizing mission.

Your Ma, a Southern swamp poet with refined sensibilities, came all the way to cold windy dusty Idaho with me, for me, and for our family too, and I promised to myself and all involved that this would work. It must work. I would do everything to make it work. I'd failed to make it work too many times before. Your Grandpa and Grandma didn't know what exactly to make of your Ma and me, but they operated with faith and hope. We had three weeks of overlap, and then it was time for them to depart. We took them to the airport. They hugged us and shook our hands and told us to raid their deep freezers, eat everything up. Then they boarded a plane and left for the middle of the Pacific Ocean.

I was not one to turn down meat. Never have been. In fact, there has never been a day in my life I've gone without it. I'm a garbage dog, and I'll eat goat just like I'll eat a rib steak just like SPAM, which is to say, until I can pick it out of my teeth. From the Idaho family freezers, your Ma and I discovered wild and domestic bounty. We retrieved ranch beef across four different years, three local 4H hams, some moose, some lamb, lots of burger and cube steak, salmon and rock fish from Alaska, and paper-wrapped elk steaks. We'd always have farm potatoes on hand, Idaho Russet Number Ones, seventy count, hand-picked from your Grandpa's cellars. Everyone who worked on the farm could take home potatoes.

Your Ma and I started taking turns, cooking it all up. Like winning the lottery. We ate meat and potatoes as much as we could stand, four nights a week, and grits and quinoa too. Avocado toast. Grapes year-round, strange new mutli-colored apples, hummus, various cheddars. Bambinos.

Burritos. Between booking and planning and executing many weddings, your Ma planted a garden with lettuce, strawberries, raspberries, onions, peas, and tomatoes. Heirloom potatoes. Everything your Ma seeded, grew. Grew like I'd never seen things grow in Idaho. Southern vines and flowers, roses of all shades and sharpness. Roses on roses. Blue spuds. She'd spend all day on summer Sundays chasing plants, fertilizing, pruning, irrigating. She knew all about bloom and yield, pistil and petal, maturation, photosynthesis.

That first year was idyllic, keeping the wedding garden and serving love on the property, though the potato harvest froze in a major weather catastrophe. Nature never had been kind up here at home. We all lived with it, lived in it, endured. The second year was a worldwide pandemic. Death abounded. We had to pause the weddings and group gatherings, but the farms kept producing, and the cattle needed pasture. The weather changed. The parties continued. The work never stopped. A drought year, hot and dry. Then a second. The earth seemed to be heaving and accelerating. Was this the long-awaited end? Or just another hiccup in the continuum?

Your Ma and I searched our souls, knowing our own gardens would soon be fallow, and we had to ask ourselves, and each other, a primal question at thirty-nine years old.

    Was there something missing?
    Someone?
    You?
    We talked it out.
    You were her idea, but I had to consider it.
    Or maybe I brought you up? I'm sure I did.
    You were on both our minds.
    How could we even? Without a miracle? Many miracles?
    My life was one big try, this being just another. Time to try again.
    So I put a wedding ring on my credit card. A big lustrous pearl set in fool's gold.
    Stuck that ring under the seat of my pickup. I wasn't going to commit to trying for a kid and not be married. Your Ma needed assurances and demonstration and a show of care. No problem for me to man up and show her.
    Turned out, the day I proposed was the afternoon after I'd broken my achilles tendon in a Thanksgiving game of basketball with my old crew of friends. Ten minutes into the game, I jogged and an ax-crack went off in my skull; my tendon snapped. I was on the hardwood. I got up and limped out to my pickup and

drove myself home to your Ma and limped my broke body into the house and proposed to her, then laid in bed unmedicated six days until surgery. I knew I was going to need her help for a long time too.

Your Ma had already bought a wedding dress, on her own credit card, the same day I bought the ring, on a Covid end-of-season internet inventory fire sale, 80% markdown. I appreciated her thriftiness and circumspection.

We were married on New Year's Day 2021, nine people in live attendance and all our family and friends out in the ether on the livestreams. A lot of love in the new year.

Then you showed up the last day, New Year's Eve 2021, in a much-needed blizzard. The accountants were thrilled at the tax break timing benefit. We were counting blessings everywhere.

I loved your Ma more than I ever loved anyone, and knew I'd love you even more than that.

We'd eaten everything out of the family freezer. We needed our own meat, now more than ever, so I knew I had to provide. With you showing up, I couldn't be relying on someone else's supply.

I put our own large coffin-style deep freezer on my credit card too.

YOUR GRANDPA

By then in his middle sixties, your Grandpa was pretty tired of my stories and shenanigans. He had raised me to ski, but I snowboarded. To farm, but instead I wandered and read. He'd hoped I'd like motorbikes and airplanes more, but I preferred histories, testimonies, secrets. We both played football, him defense and me offense, but I wrestled knowing it always bugged him, he never was a fan of the sport. I had read too much mythology and scripture not to be a wrestler. I had to grapple with the world, spur and spurn it, claim my voice in it. Fight on, never relent. Return home a victor.

Your Grandpa was a leader among men, a man of God, an organized and thorough steward of his fields and flocks. Your Grandpa controlled his behavior, his accounts, and his herds; he handled his church callings with seasoned judgement and many years of practice. Foster, as you know, means forester, caretaker of the woods. It also means caretaker of people. For this, your Grandpa was stoic, and because he'd lost his hearing so many years prior in heavy farm machinery, when he spoke, he spoke with great definition and authority. He expected a sense of order and decorum on the farm and in the church, and when he didn't receive that, he cast out the offenders from his presence, making decisions prayerfully and quickly. His rebuke was swift and sure, he never had time to waste. I'd learned that the sharp way, many times.

Along with his clear strict measure of the world were his opinions on hunting and guns. We did not have assault rifles and hallway sweepers in our home; all locked up, we had elk rifles and varmint shooters and fowl shotguns, and strict rules around those tools of death. Since I had five sisters and no brothers, your Grandpa and I bonded a lot around shooting irons. Spent a lot of time in the woods and the hills firing weapons.

Along with running lip too much and telling stories, I pushed buttons. Pressed my luck. Acted a fool. Thought I was pretty clever. I aimed my first BB gun at some new neighbor brothers who threw rocks at me and my dog. I knew the rule was to never aim a gun at another human, but I did it anyway because I could. Who would see?

Your Grandpa saw that and took my gun and

put it in the hitch slot of his farm pickup and bent my gun barrel in half. Gave it back to me with BBs dribbling out of the cracked housing, folded in two.

Many years later, after a failed marriage and a number of spectacularly failed hunts, I asked anyone in my family to aim a gun at me at a Thanksgiving shoot—an empty gun, just for research for a book I was writing. All the menfolk were out on the desert farms together, shooting yellow-bellied rock-chucks at 300 yards with a varied arsenal.

You should have seen the look of disgust on your Grandpa's face, this abhorrent request, sacrilegious. Why would I ask anyone to do that, to themselves and to myself?

A year later, to impress my second wife, I got between your Grandpa's shot path and a belligerent badger that I happened to like but that he wanted to kill. Your Grandpa couldn't shoot with me in the way, and I saw that anger and seething. He had made me take out my ponytail at the supper table. Who had he raised me to be? And who was this woman? He wanted to shoot me, I just guessed he wouldn't. He knew he was a man who lived by his own commandments, and he'd have to drop the barrel so as not to aim it at me. He did.

At thirty-three, I left for good to Texas, and your

Grandpa was so sick of my rebellion we stopped talking about hunting altogether. Stopped talking church, too, and football, and life in general. Even stopped texting, mostly. We just felt so far apart in all things. He let me go, and I left, and that was the final disagreement. We were too different to ever work together in a real way, even though that's what we'd done for so many years, bonking heads and back-talking and succeeding.

Except one morning, he called me early, panic in his voice:

"Are you okay? I dreamt that you were lost in the hills, calling out my name, but I couldn't find you."

"Dad," I said, "I'm right here, just like always."

Years later, fate, chance, and choice brought me back home, this time with your Ma. We had a lot to make up for. Your Ma returned me to Idaho, and the farm, and my father's farm desk, where he needed me to be since he was eight thousand miles away on an atoll. Trust me, I needed to be there. We had a lot going on in the family. I read his mail and signed his name and answered the bank's emails and reported the world back to him via Facebook Messenger.

On Messenger, your Grandpa and I kept things professional. When I tried to make things personal, his internet connection wouldn't quite work, or he'd always have a meeting to attend. Never could get real. Definitely skimmed my comprehensive weekly summary emails. Rarely if ever responded.

As I tended to your Grandpa's desk, I discovered a hunting program he had enrolled in: the Idaho Fish & Game's Landowner Appreciation Program. A property owner could qualify to put in on a lottery for LAP tags to cull in a later season, after the general hunts. No competition with the out-of-staters, they couldn't come so late. I'd read Idaho issued something like 22,750 tags to out-of-staters. The day the lottery opened, 66,000 applications appeared in-person and online, and crashed the State's system. The hunt was different than I remembered, high value and high stake.

Sure, I wanted to hunt, but I needed to increase my chances any way I could. Use my brain to get my meat. Those LAP tags were gold. As a landowner, your Grandpa had an option to transfer the tag to someone, right there on the form. I could go hunt a big general area, last call. In fact, I could have signed his name without his knowledge and just given myself the tag, but I'd never do that.

Via Messenger, I asked your Grandpa if I ever could purchase a LAP tag from him, and see if I could go bag the family an elk. Finally. For real this time.

17

And if he had a gun to lend me.

When he never acknowledged the message, I copied it and sent it again verbatim.

Eventually, he gave both messages a big Facebook thumbs down.

I went out and renewed my Idaho hunter license anyhow. Fish and hunt combo. I would figure it out one way or another. I had too.

His second year, I asked him the same thing again, once your Ma and I were married. Your Grandpa messaged that we'd could talk about it later, once his mission was over.

His third year, once he'd returned home and met you, held you in his arms and nuzzled your radish red head and stared into your ice blue eyes, and could see with his own hazel eyes that you were real, and I was serious; it was then that your Grandpa suggested that we call Lou for a visit and start talking in earnest about a hunt. Lou would be a better guide anyway, and your Grandpa claimed he was never hunting again, just shooting from here on out with a camera, for the sake of posterity.

LUPINE LOU

Lupine Lou was a true killer, and an old friend. How old was Lou? Timeless, it seemed, by his moustache. Eternal. He'd taken more than one Idaho wolf, as well as every other state-legal fish, fowl, and mammal. I'd witnessed more than one of his kills. Since he'd retired from the Ag Bank—where Lou and your Grandpa met and worked together many years ago, Lou bankrolling your Grandpa and his productive farms and ranches—Lou had been focusing solely on coyote eradication, texting me updates of his weekly kills. He had a goal for 500 kills a year. I could see his big white twitchy moustache in the text messages, like a wolf's snout, reporting coyote clean-ups for farmer and rancher friends on-foot and from the parachute plane. Coyotes proliferated with the growing domestic herds and flocks, gleaning calves and weaklings when operators or dogs weren't around. Probably shouldn't have been so many coyotes, but there were just so many commercial easy pickings. Lou participated in balancing that predatory population and protecting the food sources humans needed. He did not do what he did lightly. He saw it as a duty, a need. Great challenge, too.

In every month of the year, Lou had a pilot friend take him up in an ultra-lite plane where he sat saddled to the front of an aluminum frame, legs dangling open-air above the front wheel, yielding the double-barreled shotgun that had belonged to Louis, his only son.

Louis, Lou's Junior, gone too soon, departed, now among the sage angels and celestial twinkles.

Oh, how Lou notched the coyotes from above with the silver side-by-side shotgun, the pilot swooping him down in snowstorms within fifty feet of the sprinting coyote, and that's how he'd end them, click boom, click boom, pocket his empties, reload, then two more, down. Idaho Fish & Game would call Lou, too, on special missions.

Louis had been a few years younger than me, a beloved local outdoorsman who worked at Sportsman's Warehouse in Idaho Falls, at the gun counter and among the fishing poles. Louis shared all his practical and seasonal info freely, had as much hunting success as anyone I knew. Also a true killer, no doubt. Slender, sturdy, big bright eyes, an ivory smile. The kindest killer you'd ever see.

Louis once came to your Grandma's door at dusk, dressed in camo and covered in blood. Your Grandma, alone at the time, thought Louis had come to murder her, but Louis persisted in knocking, calling out your Grandma's name even, and finally she opened the door. They hadn't ever formally met. Louis needed a rifle—someone had hit a moose on the highway, and he needed the tool to put it down humanely.

Your Grandma didn't know the code to your Grandpa's gun safe, so she couldn't help Louis, but somehow he resolved the problem on the road with his knife.

Your Ma and I flew up from Houston in February 2019 to attend Louis's funeral. It was a trip home of loss and promise, great pain and the unknown future. It all hurt, cold to the bone. I was pained to see Lupine Lou, my mighty friend, stiff upper lip, grieving with his wife and daughter. We sat front-row for Louis's services, the day glistening and bitter and dead-ache.

I did not know what to expect from Lou, facing the nightmare of speaking at his only son's services. Wrenching; boggling; unfathomable. I never could imagine him weeping, nor your Grandpa. They do not shed tears. They contain themselves. They keep it together. This, in part, was what made them so deadly. Clear-eyed, they could always target and trigger. I was always different. Inside and outside, I gnashed and wailed, long before I even had you, at the pain of loss. How do we keep going? How do we survive? Why does everything good die?

Lou choked up while talking, of course, but he proceeded to tell a story of how one day he got Louis in a predicament that almost cost him everything much too soon.

If I recall it right—if I can do it justice—it will never be as good as Lou's true version—the story was this:

The family used to have pack-mules that they would take up to Leadore to hike and camp and hunt, Lou and his wife Judy and the kids Michelle and Louis, both under fifteen. Stark, harsh mountains, and a howling wind. I've hunted geese up there with Lou and your Grandpa, just under the cemetery. Coffin blinds, semi-auto shotguns, buried in snow fields. Lou has shown so many so much of the world, starting with his family. But they did it primitively, not easy family camping, but dirt-living with mules and canvas tents up in the crags and cliffs.

They'd been up there a time and finally came

down and headed back to town, all four of them in a single-cab pickup with a bed full of gear and gets, pulling a horse-trailer with four sweaty mules. They left because of the heat, the summer baking the hillsides, thermals rising off the rock and lava desert stretches, drought. No air conditioning in the cab of the pickup, and they were campfire rank and running hot. They pulled off at Gilmore Summit to let the truck cool down, and Lou invited Louis—or maybe convinced him?—or maybe Louis wanted some air?—I can't totally recall—but no matter the sequence, what finally happened was that Lou unloaded young Louis's bike from the truck, and set it pointed downhill, a long and gradual many-miles-long decline into the northwest side of the Upper Snake River Valley.

Louis quickly mounted the bike and coasted down the slope. Poor Judy, of course, had not been included in the decision, and was fuming at the reality. Lou loaded up in the pickup quickly and got after his boy, catching up. Lou picked up speed—downhill and with a trailer of mules, mind you—10, 15, 20, 25, 30—trying to stay close to Louis, who was not wearing a helmet and gaining distance on the old pickup, boots off the pedals, the tires smoking.

With every increased mile-per-hour on that

speedometer, Lou tightened both hands on the wheel and did everything he could to hurry; with every mile faster, Judy squeezed onto Michelle, and the dashboard. With every tick up, the temperature in the cab went down a degree, and they were all freezing. The look that Judy gave Lou froze his blood. He had never been colder. Louis was truly on his own, and the rest of the family was powerless. Ice ran through their hearts.

All Lou could do was watch Louis roll away.

Here was the miracle: Louis, somehow, rode it out. He never faltered, he never put his feet down and got out of balance, he kept perfect grip, stayed centered on the seat, and found a way to slow down at some point and safely stop. The family was collected and reunited and back in the pickup alive together again.

Louis lived so many rich years after that. Then suddenly he was gone, his tag called and notched. The loss certainly changed the resonance of the hunt, and we hadn't called Lou about going out since the funeral, going on three years.

It was a big deal to call Lou up and have him answer. I told him what was up and asked him if he'd come out on an elk hunt for me and my family, and he said yes straightaway. I swore I could hear his mustache. He lit in on a list of preparations, telling me to start training that very day, build deep arm strength, deep lung strength, dry-fire my rifle a few times.

"But Lou," I said, "I don't even have a gun."

That was true. I'd never owned a gun big enough for elk, and like your Grandma, was not privy to the combination to your Grandpa's gun safe.

I had part-ownership in a rifle with your outlaw snowboarder Uncle Nate, a Remington 700 that fired 300 ultra magnums, but Nate had it in Montana. Or Utah? I didn't know where he was. I'd bought half-in on it and he drove it up from Utah and I held it through a court case of his, so the state couldn't confiscate it. He'd beaten the case and taken the gun back and kept it moving down the road.

I muttered again at my lack of firepower, unsure of what to do.

Lou cleared his throat and spoke up:

"A rifle is our last concern. Use a broom, or a ski pole. A two-by-four. Pull up, sight down the line, visualize it. Your elk is out there. Do you see it? I do."

ME

July 2022— my fortieth year on earth, your first— was the month that your Grandpa and Lou and I all agreed that we would go out on an elk hunt. That month, I published my first book too. Your Ma and I did it together, like pretty much everything at this point. You were seven months old at the time. I had a lot more to worry about beyond a fall elk hunt that may or may not materialize. It was a long way off. We had weddings every weekend, and I had farm work all the days I didn't have weddings, and we were also establishing a book company. We had you and your siblings to raise and feed too.

I was old, and felt it, healing slow in the foot. Just before my birthday, we'd finally taken our turn with the coronavirus, even though your Ma and I had had two rounds of the vax and the booster. Hit us at the start of our busiest wedding week—five events across seven days—and your Ma laid in bed and nursed you and agonized silently and handled all the guests via text and video recordings sent from her bed. Your older siblings and I would go out in the darkness, early morning and late at night, alone but masked, and clean the property and reset and redecorate for the next wedding. I felt worse than that time I was electrocuted. You never languished a day through that, you were fine, but as we recovered, my body writhed in pain, such discomfort in my shoulders and knees and back that I could hardly walk straight and upright. It hurt to use my arms. It all hurt. I hurt so bad I couldn't remember what feeling good felt like.

For months this pain persisted, and after I'd worked through all the home-remedies and OTC ointments, I started seeking care. I visited a massage therapist, then a chiropractor dually credentialed for humans and horses—he bought one of my paperbacks, then a doctor's office, then a pain clinic. There they injected my joints with magic medicine. Finally some help. With that slight relief, I started working with a Physical Therapist named Chad who had just opened up shop three days a week in Ririe, our little farming hamlet of less than a thousand people, and I could visit when the farm was slow in the afternoon. I stretched and exercised and tried to regain my strength and breath, but the healing came slower than ever before.

I explained the LAP tag and my motivation to Chad, and he told me about his disabled father who shot a deer at five hundred yards while sitting in the driver's seat of his specialized rig, taking wind and shot coordinates from another son who was spotting through a military sniper's scope. If he could do that, maybe I could get better and get out there. I had my doubts, didn't say much to your Grandpa or Lou.

My life had been too much recovery, this fact clear to me at forty. I had wasted so much time trying too hard, sending it too big, injuring myself, then having to sit out and heal. A Nineties Comeback Story, stuck in the training montage. I read too many adventure books as a kid. They made me want to be something notable, someone great, someone that was worth a story. I wanted to go out in the world, scale up its face and come down shredding. I was strong, fast, fierce and could run as long as I wanted to—until I broke something. I always took myself out. The body imperfect and weak. My imagination outsizing my ability. Me contorting and crashing and busting a bone, then stuck laying up.

Per Lou's hunter's training, I laid in bed and ate beef jerky, flexing my green-healed tendon, trying to trick my brain into thinking about elk. I reached back in memory to another early hunt in the Antelope

Hills, when your Grandpa dropped me and my cousin at the bottom of a long draw covered in black timber. Me and my cousin had our pellet guns, and were ready to pop some pine hens. They were dumb and great to eat. Your Grandpa instructed us to walk up into the timber and follow the cattle trail up and pick our way up to the sagebrush flat, where they'd all be waiting and stationed for any spooked elk. He clunked off quietly and slowly up the hill on the far side, turned his headlights off in the breaking dawn dark, and my cousin and I started in and up.

In the timber, the temperature dropped, and we could see each other's breath. We could walk with such stealth up there, I felt invisible, and we stayed parallel to each other from about ten feet away and stepped carefully through grass and branch and bough, needles and cowpies cushioning every footfall. The trees creaked and bent from a breeze high up, and my own swallow sounded amplified and strange. My cousin and I moved soft and fleet. We'd hunted canal birds and chased cows our whole lives.

Deep in, we came to a clearing, and in that clearing, we encountered a herd of a dozen or so cow elk, bedded down. Long necks up, heads alert, ears orbiting. My cousin and I stopped. What were these creatures? We really had no idea. We'd never been up close to elk. But weren't these deer? A gang of Mulies? No antlers in the whole harem, but ears like satellites. Their breath in the clearing made it noticeably warmer, and the elk stayed down, not moving, while we crept around their edges and kept walking up.

We got to the top and out in the sagebrush, and walked out into the visible plain for a hundred yards when three pickups converged on us and your Grandpa got out of one of them and started grilling us. We told them of the herd of deer, but after reporting the description of the dark hide and the long snouts, of course that had been the very elk we were meant to harvest, and everyone went charging quietly into the trees and headed down the draw, barrels first.

My cousin and me, exhausted and chagrined, stayed at the pickups, and heard no volley of shots, no targets, zero chance. They saw the matted grass though, felt their heat, smelled them, but we never did find them again that season.

Beef jerky could never be elk jerky, I realized, so I had to try again. I had to hunt. I still had strength enough. I worked hard in that little gym, followed Chad's orders, and imagined elk up in the Antelope Hills. Did I see them? No. I served weddings and surveyed acres, took you choring, and made your Ma's first book.

All of that helped me beat my pain. That, and my imagination.

Still never have hurt bad enough to stop, or stay down long, either.

ANOTHER WEIRD YEAR

All your life to this point, we had been in the drought, hot and dry and no precipitation from two thin winters. The aquifer was drawn down, and we were digging the farm wells deeper, no easy or cheap feat. The canals ran just a few inches, and the reservoirs where we crawfished were down to the very bottom crease of the ravine, capacity at less than twenty percent. We'd never seen it this dry. That year your Grandpa's dirt was pulverized, no sub-moisture anywhere at all, the barley short, the spuds smallish, misshapen. A weird, water-starved crop. Green hay was like gold. The smallest and most valuable crop in history. This ugly harvest would all be eaten up, with nothing to spare. We on the crew handled the crop like precious, delicate loot.

We harvested the grains in August. Lou started scouting the Antelope Hills for elk. Never saw a thing. Too hot. They were still up high. Then we got digging the potatoes in September, sort of. The potato plants wouldn't die. They persisted, even in the second year of a drought, green-feeding, trying to get any suck of water they could. We dug an extra ten days longer than usual, the weather sunny and summer-like. Planted all the acres of fall wheat, easy and steady. The potatoes were eggs and nubbins, nothing more, yields down forty percent.

In October, the first LAP tag opened, and Lou went up to the high country alone, but never found elk there either. They were really high up, room and temps to roam. They didn't come down to the Antelope Hills. Those elk, my elk, up in the highest shade, munching on clover and sweet grass, drinking from the slightest melt. Safe and sound. The fall wheat had an unexpected growth spurt in the mild weather, and was four inches tall.

In November, once we finished the spuds and brought the cattle herds down from the picked-over and yellowed ranch pastures, I asked your Grandpa if he thought we'd get the hunt. Your Grandpa looked tongue-tied, but said he had changed his plans and would be going to Hawaii soon, for an indefinite amount of time. Said he missed the sting of sea-water in his nose. He also cited that we hadn't seen any elk sign or scat during the cattle roundup, how weird. Where were the elk? Your Grandpa told me to count him out. Like he said, he wasn't a hunter anymore anyhow. Maybe I didn't even know who your Grandpa was anymore. We were all always changing.

As the days of the month added up, I recalibrated my expectations. If the hunt happened, it would be the payoff of two years of negotiations and thirty-eight years of practice, and likely just be me and Lou. If it didn't, it would just be like every other year before it, and so I gained or lost nothing. It would have all been an exercise in imagination, nothing more.

The week before Thanksgiving, though, brought an Arctic Blast down from the North, and the weather shifted cold and wet, and by Wednesday we'd gotten an inch of new snow, a nice welcome change. We celebrated Thanksgiving that year at the wedding venue with two other artist friends and more snow. We talked and rapped and played board games. I burned the gravy, and the turkey was dry—but that's why I cooked a mustard ham too. Potatoes were perfect, lumps for texture. We ate fat and happy, including yourself. We stomped and tromped around the dance floor singing Disney songs from the Nineties, a common language, I guess.

You were teething then, had your two front teeth, and your two bottom teeth, and one half of your next tooth on the bottom too. Every day you were a different kind of ornery cuss, and we tried ice rings and popsicles and chew toys but found no relief. You found sustenance in my turkey and ham, I helped you tear at it with your little chompers, like hydraulic presses with no regulators, just full-force opened and closed. I had to be careful so you wouldn't catch my fingertips with your bite. I wasn't sure if you'd ever figure it out. Then it snowed all day Black Friday too. We hadn't seen consecutive-day steady precip like this in two years.

Saturday, the snow stopped, temps clear and cold, and Lou texted me to inform that a large herd of elk had moved onto the Antelope Hills. Eighty or so happened to be parked on the hillside belonging to your Grand Uncle Brad, a man I was quite fond of, the older brother to your Grandpa, also a farmer and rancher. So I called up your Grand Uncle Brad to get the full scoop. He answered me first ring. I asked if it was true, and sure enough, eighty elk were eating the radish tops off a late-plant cover crop option they were trying out to save some moisture.

"I have a LAP tag," I said to Brad, "Could I have your permission?"

There was a pause on the phone while I heard Brad walk into another room. He was over seventy years old then, emeritus from the church, wealthy, powerful, and had broken his foot in a ranch accident. He still worked every day. I had heard he was walking around in a hard plastic protective boot, out there in the corrals. I could hear him thumping the boot on his hardwood floors, dragging it.

"Come pick me up! We'll go up there right now! I'll show you how to jump them! We'll get you your first elk, just you wait, and we'll beat my sons-in-law to them too!"

Maybe he was emboldened by some post-surgery opiates? I was not opposed to the plan. It sounded like an adventure I'd enjoy.

"Do you have a gun we can use?" I asked him.

He scoffed and chuckled.

"You don't have a gun?"

Before he cut the call, he said—

"Figure it out, I'm ready as soon as you are."

You and me and your Ma drove the guests down-and-back to Salt Lake City on Sunday, and on our return leg of the drive, your Uncle Jordan called me up. He too was a farmer and a dead-eye hunter who had land adjacent to us and to Brad. Your Uncle Jordan had married your Aunt Abby, my youngest sister, going on ten years ago now. Jordan was soon to coach the Ririe Bulldogs to a basketball district championship too. He was a guy who didn't mess around, had taken game in two continents.

Your Uncle Jordan informed me that the elk had departed Brad's fields and were now on his place. He offered to me the great privilege of shooting my first elk off of his hay and grass, which he had fertilized, watered, and harvested with great care every year mostly just for an opportunity such as this.

I was too proud to ask Jordan to lend me his rifle, knowing he would happily oblige and say yes, maybe even take me up there and scope me in. He was a true killer too, and generous. I said I planned to talk to Lou and get something in the books and would let him know if we needed access. He said he'd await the good news.

With all the news and action, I figured I should call Lou once I finally got off the Interstate. Almost back home, my back seizing and aching from the seven hours in the car in, winter driving conditions the whole way, a group text pinged on my phone, and of all people, it was your Grandpa, Lou, and Me. It was Sunday night. Your Grandpa would be leaving for Hawaii Wednesday morning.

Your Grandpa texted:
Hunt On Tomorrow Morning Shop 5:45 AM
Lou sent the Thumbs Up Emoji.
I dang near ran off the road, but didn't, not in the

all-wheel drive wagon your Ma drives. We got that car to keep us all safe on these winter roads.

GO BAG

Out the basement window of our basement apartment, big fat flakes kept falling eye level. It felt like we were already neck deep in snow. Home, sweet home. The hunt was on, and your Grandpa was coming. He never could turn down an elk hunt. Maybe we knew each other after all.

I didn't know how we'd get up on anything with snowfall like this. It was coming down heavy enough they might not even have the roads plowed.

I finally texted the group back:

Gonna be the best road hunt of all time

I regretted saying that, noting that a mention of a road hunt would sour any real hunter's mood and possibly jinx us. We didn't want it easy. I tried to regain some ground by sending out a link to Tobias Wolff's short story "Hunters in the Snow." Neither of them responded to either message.

Having screwed that up, I walked back to the bedroom, laid down, and read the short story on my phone, was surprised and tickled by all the aspects

I'd forgotten, and wondered how your Grandpa would feel about that dang sad dog, and why Toby had to do that. After a minute, imagining both those men would be disappointed in my lethargy and time-waste, I jumped up and started sorting through my belongings to get ready.

I went into the storage room and retrieved all three pairs of the snowshoes, and fished out from a pile of insulated black boots, the pair I thought were mine. My pair I'd had for twenty years, buy-it-for-life Sorels. Instead, unbeknownst to me, I grabbed the wrong pair, one inherited from your Ma's cousin from Nebraska who had a stint living in Alaska but moved back home and no longer needed deep winter gear, so sent it to us.

A lesser pair for me, surely, but at the time, I couldn't see the difference, I had the blood fever, and let the adrenaline make my selections. I had to hurry and get ready now.

I took down my duffel bag and threw in the Xmas hatchet that your Uncle Nate gave me, a handsome tool. We had a matching pair, sharp and well-weighted. I paid for both of them, and that was fine with me. I threw in my skinning knife and bone saw combo, scabbarded together in leather. I'd found that abandoned in your Grandpa's old office desk.

Got out the seven-shooter revolver, a .17 for varmints, I guess, or maybe a mountain lion attack? I didn't know; it was the only close handy gun. I'd rather have it than come empty handed. I checked the revolver's action first, rolled the chamber, made sure nothing was live, strapped it back up safely and set it in the bag.

I turned to the closet and started strategizing clothes. Layered up. Good thick action boxer briefs, knee-high socks, and another short ankle sock over those. Green for luck, any chance I could, for superstition. Insulated jeans, a long-sleeved thin workout shirt, a dark henley over that. A thick reflective hunting flannel, my green denim wool-lined vest, and my rabbit skinned bomber hat I'd had since high school, still my favorite hunting hat, my fat head barely fitting. Last, I needed shooting gloves, and the best I could find was a sleek black pair of neoprene mitten liners for snowboarding.

I hadn't bathed for two days, lounging in the holiday and not doing much, and I realized I felt fat and stuffed and a bit rotten. The drive hadn't helped. No mighty hunter here. My back hurt and my shoulder pain had only gotten worse. I stunk, and my fingernails and toenails were two weeks too long.

Part of me thought to freshen up. I decided

that tonight wouldn't be the night. I had lived long enough to know that changing something small right before something big can cause the wrong kind of interference and conflict. I would not shave, scrub, brush, clip, or wash. I needed all my natural weaponry and musk.

I wanted to be ripe, fetid, reek of the earth, wear ragged nails and bear sharp teeth. Figured your Ma wouldn't mind. Her soul was muddy from swamps and black-tea rivers, and deep cerulean Bay blue. She had been salty and gritty, hunting snakes and birds and squirrels. She knew how to be sneaky and venomous, and also how to effectively check for ticks. Truly, your Ma was perfect for me.

Your Ma came in the bedroom and saw me dudded up, ready to go make a kill. She licked her lips. Boy howdy, did she love me. She slow-stepped around the bed and sidled up to me and unbuckled the latch of my rabbit-skinned hat holding down my ear flaps, removed it and tossed it on the mattress.

"Hey there, Mister," she said.

I didn't have to say much, I said less.

She unzipped my vest, then went button by button, zipper and fastener, layer by layer. It took her some time, because I'd been thorough and choosy in my selection of snow hunt layers, so I stood there for a while. Soon enough, she had me down to bare skin except for my four socks.

I was direly exposed, pleasantly rank, horizontal. Just what she wanted.

That's how I fell asleep, too, once it was sleeping time, your Ma curled beside me under the hand-me-down quilts.

RENDEVOUS

I woke at 4:00 AM, then 4:29, 4:30, 4:43, then 4:49. At 4:56, I got out of bed and re-layered on all my hunting clothes that were strewn across the bedroom. Your mother didn't stir; which was fine, she could sleep. I'd heard all about how much she loved me, I had no doubts. I peed in the toilet and didn't brush my teeth, closed the bedroom door quietly, then I came to your room.

You were there, asleep on your bed, face-down, cute little butt in the air. A onesie with footies. Sucking your thumb. Temperature just right, your mobile not moving at all. I was lucky I got to see you every morning, live or in the monitor or through the app. I watch you any chance I can. I had scooped you up so many mornings to take you to the warm side of your Ma. She slept so soundly because she always stayed up late with you, and I always stayed up late with her, but I never could stay in bed for more than five hours anyway. Who can afford to sleep in? There was always so much to do for love, or the farm, or the books. So much hay to make.

    I watched you snooze, your little body rising and sighing, and started my pickup via the app. Seat heaters too. Toasted it all up. Defrosted it. Closed your door ever so quietly, made it out of the apartment and to the backdoor ramp that led up and out to my pickup. Threw in all my snowshoes and go bag next to your car seat—I've been bringing you to work at Grandpa's farm since you were an infant, where I kept you on the floor under my desk; I've brought you to work since the day you could ride in a truck. I brushed off all the windows and lights with the snow brush.

    Outside, four more fresh new inches of wet snow. In the bottom of the valley we'd gotten a foot and a half of snow so far. The air still so wet it smelled like we were by the sea, which, of course, we were not. We were in the desert. It had been a drought for two years. This wet air smelled lush and fresh. Heavy duty petrichor. I loaded my gear in the backseat. Big, wet flakes, temp maybe thirty-five degrees. I marveled at them falling. No leaving our basement apartment easily that day, especially with me going hunting and not shoveling you out. Cleaning my pickup made me a little queasy, the early morning actions of it. Maybe I'd given a little too much thanks that week, the first Thanksgiving with you? Partied a little too hard? Or was I covid sick, or some other new deadly virus?

I felt enthused, but not tip-top. I put the truck in four-wheel drive and made fresh tracks out to the road, the night still deep-dark, visibility maybe twenty feet in the yellow headlights, snow falling consistently. Quiet everywhere but in my head. Couldn't keep my thoughts still.

I put on a song, "Wolf Like Me" by TV On The Radio, and listened to that a couple of times, and went about thirty-five mph in the center of the road. Not even the plows were out on County Line yet, though I'd heard them on the highway exchange. Nothing out in the country though. The empty canals along the road were filled up with snow.

When that song ended and I'd repeated it once, I listened to the cover "Wolf Like Me" by Local H. I sang that one harder, imagining myself a wolf, and head-banged a little too viciously. Had to roll down the window. Threw up all down my truck.

Then I played "Wolf Like Me" by Shovels & Rope, and got sentimental but not for long, because by then I was to Ririe and your Grandpa's farm office and thinking about you.

I parked there and let myself inside and puked in

the toilet and cleaned myself up. I went out and to my desk and got my Idaho State hunter's license and LAP tag out of the top drawer, and headed back out.

Before I could open the door, I heard your Grandma call down from above:

"Good luck, you mighty hunter!"

"Aloha, Mom, thank you," I hollered back through the two-way vent. At that time, your Grandpa and Grandma lived above the farm office in a one-bedroom apartment. They were like devils and angels, always around, something I'd accepted and been fine about. I'd rather have them than not. I knew she was upstairs awake on her computer, completing genealogy for the church. She started and ended and lived all her days for the dead and gone.

I started shoveling the front sidewalk, and while I did that, your Grandpa pulled up in his pickup. Your Grandpa asked me if he could buy me breakfast at Maverik, the gas station where we'd been eating bad breakfast all our lives. I said a sausage biscuit. He pulled across to the store. His pickup looked a lot like mine, but newer and different and better. Both Ford Powerstroke F-150 diesels, the last of their kind. He got his after I got the one I drive. He bought both of them. They're farm pickups, built for work but driven everywhere by us. Our whole lives in white pickups, with our notebooks and knives, first-aid kit and extra gear, tools and chains, bags of jerky, canned caffeine, guns, shovels, families.

    Before I had the sidewalk finished, your Grandpa had returned and tossed me the sandwich. I stood at his window and took a bite. Your Grandpa had been tanning then for three days straight in preparation for a trip with your Grandma to Hawaii. He glowed like a red potato, and his teeth shined like coconut flesh. Otherwise, it was dark out.

    "How do you feel?" your Grandpa asked me.

    "I have my doubts in weather like this," I said, snow falling on my tongue, "but I want to try."

    "I don't know what we'll do, but Lou will," your Grandpa said. "He always does. Let's go."

    I got in my pickup and trailed your Grandpa out of town and up the hill and onto the highway, then off through the farms. On the lonely highway, a pickup pulled in not twenty seconds behind us, and sure enough, that was Lou. We drove for five or so miles then turned off the highway and onto the county road and got to the shop. All parked in a line in front of the green metal shop building your Great Grandpa built. Faded metal, it'd been here sixty years, serviced a lot of tractors, facilitated a lot of crops. I started here, pulling weeds and sweeping floors and arranging nuts and bolts.

We all got out and followed your Grandpa inside as he turned on all the lights. We stood in the bay with a newly painted Peterbilt semi that the farm guys were working on. New farm color scheme: Black, Silver, and Green. A chrome bumper the size of a railroad tie, and two silver exhaust stacks. A heavenly creature. So nice your Grandpa wouldn't let anyone drive it but himself. Two key guys, Cowboy Kent and Operator Andrew, headed up the re-brand, and it was turning out aces, something the neighbors would talk about.

Lou and your Grandpa talked more than usual, excited about the weather. Two long dry years of drought, now look at this moisture. Moisture was what we worried all year long and prayed for. All three of us took it as prayers answered; the snow adding water to our basins and catches and aquifer.

No reason to complain. Now if we could just find the elk.

The two old dogs volleyed back and forth about the markets, the mission, the good life. I took note of your Grandpa's outfit: just jeans, an orange and gray Klim snowmachine coat, and an Andean style alpaca beanie your Aunt Sydnee had brought him when she was on a service mission in an orphanage in Ecuador.

Thin leather work boots too. The three years on his island mission had taken the weather from your Grandpa's face, and he clearly had forgotten how to dress for cold. He wore jandals too many days.

Lou, on the other hand, in insulated rubber boots, thick green wool slacks, a gray wool button-up coat, a black vest visible underneath, and a stately, large, lush mustache that twitched dang near from ear to ear. Lupine Lou was the wolf-man, prepared for all elements and any challenge.

"How do you feel?" Lou asked me slyly.

"Ready," I lied.

ROAD HUNT

We exited your Great Grandpa's shop into a full whiteout. The white wet flakes filled the still-dark sky like plentiful moths. Couldn't see anything in that white wall. Quiet too, with the snow dampening everything. Feet, undisturbed. The snow field unbroken through the yard, past the cellars, to the fields and the dark. Snow: A sea. A desert. A void. All that green fall wheat, snowed under too.

We opted not to take your Grandpa's F-150, nor mine. A true pleasure to throw the snowshoes and the duffel into Lou's little silver four-door Toyota Tacoma TDR with the action shell. All sorts of cool stuff in the back, all puzzled in, our gear thrown in on top. I couldn't tell if it was Lou's or Louis's. They both had identical trucks, same year, same mileage. Of course, Lou used both of them.

I took the backseat and had to move Lou's day-pack across the seat onto his overnighter pack, then pulled out two rifles and leaned them up in the middle. Squeezed in there, in the dark, while the two captains got in up front, Lou driving. None of us buckled up, and the side windows immediately fogged. Lou's headlights needed a good bleach bath, one pointed up and one pointed sideways. The flakes came down fast and furious, the Toyota's wipers whipped, and the defroster blew hard to beat our hot bad breath. We backed out and squared up and headed for the Dam Road, and saw another pickup cross our headlights, headed towards the Dam.

Only three days left for the hunting season, and we weren't the only ones with LAP tags. Everyone owned land out here, who knew who we were hunting alongside? Or how many? Seeing that other truck shut us up. We got behind in its tracks and followed its faint red taillights down the road. A pickup pulled off the highway and got in our tracks, headlights dim back there somewhere in the snow, a lame road hunt train.

I broke that fraught silence, leaned up in the space from the backseat:

"Who did their homework last night?"

Meaning, the Tobias Wolff story. Had they read?

Neither confirmed or denied from up front.

"Huh," I said. "Now you'll never know which one of us gets shot."

Somehow the two up front said even less.

I looked out the foggy window and bit my lip. Thought about your Ma, imagined her sleeping. Tried to take a picture of the snow with my phone. Didn't work. Lou and your Grandpa talked about beef and grain prices, gas prices, the spud shortage, the coyote hunts. Into the two weird cones of yellow we drove, snow still coming, snow crunching under us, snow everywhere except the black void of the empty Ririe Reservoir, which was built to catch the snow. At nineteen percent capacity, as low as any of us have ever seen it, the dam had plenty of room to catch and fill.

Our family history was water in the desert. We'd been seeing the dam our whole lives, marking its level, waterskiing and fishing on it, me and your Grandpa and all our family members. Your Great Grandpa saw it before us, when there wasn't a dam, it was just the Willow Creek Canyon, a sharp and steep watershed. Willow Creek had historically been prone to flood all the way to Eagle Rock, washing out plenty of settlers and flooding all the dirt basements.

Your Great Grandpa started this farm with his family. Uncles got him into his first purchase. It was dry land then. The Fifties, and the pumping irrigation technology had just reached the Snake River Valley, and dry ash and loam activated with transported water that made great and plentiful crops. A new fertile crescent from Wyoming to Washington. The canals diverted from the Snake River fed the valleys since the late eighteen hundreds, but how to irrigate the hills, so rich and fertile? How to water the good west desert dirt? If you could do that, you could really make taters.

Your Great Grandpa figured out how to irrigate the hills and grew potatoes. It was a farm accident that caused his early demise. He got pinned between the cellar's dirt wall and a loaded spud truck. Brakes went out, and he couldn't get out of the way. Your Great Grandpa survived that, even though he was trapped back there for four or five minutes, all the crew trying to take whatever pressure off they could until they could chain up a tractor to drag off the truck. As far as I know, your Great Grandpa didn't even go to the hospital that night. Kept working. But that's what got him. Lasting internal damage to his kidneys.

The accident caused various health problems, and he had to be hospitalized a lot for treatments in Idaho Falls and Salt Lake City. Like any potato farmer worth their leather gloves, your Great Grandpa operated his acres from the hospital bed via your Great Grandma from ages forty to forty-four.

The Reclamation Act happened in 1972, and new government funding and projects became available. One of those was damming Willow Creek, but it was your Great Grandpa who owned all the way to the dead-end turnout of the road where everyone pulled off to throw their old garbage off the cliff to the creek.

The farm started pretty much as a dump, and so did the dam. But all of a sudden, the Federal Government was sending your Great Grandpa letters asking for easement through the turnout and down the cliff to the dam site. They needed to start foundational work as soon as they could.

Your Great Grandpa would only make the deal if, along with fair compensation, the Federal Government would allow his two sons to keep a boat down on the site that only they could access. For waterskiing and fishing. The Feds agreed, in exchange for use of a tractor plow implement they could use to level their work.

Later, when your Great Grandpa was out of the hospital and up at the farm to work, when your Grand Uncle Brad was on his first early mission to Texas, Spanish-Speaking, and your Grandpa was just eleven or twelve years old, your Grandpa would go out to the farm with your Great Grandpa, and your Great Grandpa would take him out to the edge of the farm at the rim of the canyon, and leave your Grandpa on a high rocky perch, and tell your Grandpa to keep a keen eye on the workers down below, building the dam line by line, every day inching it taller, using their plow. He'd leave your Grandpa out on the canyon rim with a bag of apples and a .22 rifle, telling him to count the passes and to listen for rattlesnakes. The dam building displaced a large population of diamondbacks, so many that the tractor operators were finding them diced and wrapped in the implements. Grandpa learned how to shoot them young too, out there on water watch, eating apples and counting. We all know how to listen for them too, because of him.

With your Grandpa left up on that ledge, your Great Grandpa would go work in his tractor, tending to his farm. Turning dirt requires total attention, and lots of diesel and hours. You have to pay attention and keep your rows straight, and realize that every acre, every foot, matters.

Your Grandpa watched your Great Grandpa pass away. Going through this forged him and your Grand Uncle into a stubborn, relentless, righteous duo. They brought the whole family to work, the wives and mothers, in the kitchens and the offices, and me and my sisters and cousins too, with the men out getting dirty and crappy, sun-up to sun-down. The brothers also tended to the church, serving, teaching and leading, and were generally well-respected, but sometimes envied and resented.

The church put up a monument to your Great Grandpa near the softball fields to the east of Pioneer Cemetery. All black porous lava rock, black basalt, but with a big solid white and silver glistening granite inlay right above the plaque for his name and memorial. Fitting, I've always thought. That white rock stuck in the middle of the lava. What did it all mean? Symbolize? Was your Great Grandpa purer than normal? I'd always wanted to meet the man in the flesh. Instead, I'd only ever seen him in paranormal spiritual manifestation, a story I'll tell you another day.

I worked the farm young, pulling weeds and picking up pop cans and sweeping the shop. Your Grandpa and your Grand Uncle had all the fields on this side of the Reservoir—and everything on that far side of the Dam too, matter of fact. I guess they kind of had it all. They'd carved out and irrigated fertile potato and grain farms, horse-trading and buying and selling up. In doing so, they had acquired good contiguous swaths with excellent ground water, and developed proficient pumped irrigation systems using miles of buried mainline and above-ground irrigation pivots. They made the desert bloom. They'd ventured into niche markets beyond beef cattle and hay and potatoes; veal calves, for a few years, I remember, I hand-fed them, and certified seed potatoes, and many more.

    Big vision and grit, these dusty brothers that were also your blood, filling and emptying potato cellars, hauling cows across four Idaho counties and into Montana and Wyoming, these Bishops and Stake Presidents, these honorable, ornery cusses. I'd seen them both so angry they jumped on their hats flat. I've been known to zing a hat over a fence, scream at a tree. When it was time for your Grandpa to no longer work with your Grand Uncle, well, I was there for that, and they handled it as well as two business partners and family members could. Split everything as fairly and as legally as it warranted. Stayed civil and generous with each other.

    I stayed with your Grandpa. That was a given. I have been pretty much here ever since, except for when I wasn't, but even then, I was always writing about it, right here by the Dam, dreaming of rattlesnakes and wakeboarding, the green potato fields, the golden stands of malt barley, the mirror surface of the water, the depths, the crayfish, all the garbage that's come and gone.

We passed the Juniper Boat Ramp and traveled down the decline, crunching the snow.

The rig ahead of us, much more meaty, got to the bottom of the decline and started climbing out of it—the road changing from pavement to gravel there, Meadow Creek Road—and took a minute but made it out. Red taillights disappeared up and over.

Down in the bottom of the wash, the reservoir behind and below us, we lost some momentum. A slow rally up. The speedometer didn't move past five mph, the needles hovering. Couldn't pull us up, spun out. Lou backed down his tracks, backed up and out of the decline to the pavement, and turned around. The pickup behind us had disappeared, and again we were alone.

I thought about the dark lake, about trapping crawfish out there with you and your Ma and your siblings and our dogs, pulling up mudbugs to boil with the garden potatoes. Captaining the 1991 Duckworth, a twenty-one-foot aluminum jet boat that we kept on the farm in an empty cellar, bought at an auction of fleet vehicles by Idaho Power Company, of course it was your Grandpa who spotted and nabbed the buy.

We celebrated your Southern heritage trapping

crawdads. Those tasty, succulent morsels of muscle, like snow melt and plowed dirt, the sweat and blood off the farm, satisfying after the hard work.

I'd written the book here so many times in my mind; even still, in the madrugada on the Dam Road, everything was blanketed, eerie, new one more time.

I could never do the whole story justice, as the story was always changing faster than I could write.

WHEN IN DOUBT

Lou trucked us slowly back towards the farm shop, snowfall not abating. I wondered if we'd pull in and give up, but we didn't.

"With precip like this," Lou said, "the farmers are off to a great start, at least."

"An answer to prayers," your Grandpa said, for the fourth time.

Nothing more important to pray for but water, except maybe the missionaries, and meat in the freezer.

We were a prayerful family, and a prayerful people. Ask and ye shall receive. I had really been getting into prayer as I was trying for my first big kill, back at fifteen. Three years beyond the first legal age to kill. A cringy fact. In Idaho, any good hunter killed their first at twelve years old. We just hadn't had any luck on my hunts. I didn't really have a middle volume, and I only very selectively deployed my quiet volume. I couldn't sit still. I wanted to run through the forest, touch every tree, chase the pine chickens, hear them thumping in the brush, build a fire, send smoke signals, find the neighbor girl.

So your Grandpa and I had been skunked three years, and had lost some hunting buddies and community cred on those hunts, but still your Grandpa was trying with me, and I with him, neither of us the type to relent. Girls were starting to ask if I was gonna get my deer—the situation was getting embarrassing. I'd do anything to score.

September 1997: fifteen in Idaho, the first year I had a legal license. I drove a 1965 Ford F-100, practiced football twice a day at Rigby High School, once early in the morning, and once after school, and any other times I was at the farm helping in grain harvest, usually unloading grain trucks into a grain bin. Your Grandpa, as always, drove the lead combine, and for a week he'd been up high in the Antelope Hills, and had seen more than once a big muley buck, rutting about with does.

So your Grandpa and I planned it, and one afternoon as soon as football was out, I drove all the way from the high school to the dry farm hills and found him in a combine with a rifle. I changed into some hunting gear and took the gun and your Grandpa laid it all out.

The buck right now resided on the other side of

the rocky point. If I picked a position right here in the draw, he'd walk up and around and through and push them my way. All I had to do was sit and wait.

No one was with me, so I couldn't talk to anyone, this also part of your Grandpa's plan. Eliminate all obstacles and distractions.

As the sun got low in the west, your Grandpa took off through the stubble, around the trees and rocks, moving quickly and controlled. Always watching the hillside for movement. Weird to see him without his gun.

I had your Grandpa's gun. An open-sight 25.06 with an engraved wood stock, four shells in the stock magazine and nothing in the chamber. A very successful gun. I'd been here for some hunts and heard about the rest. I found a shady spot on the far side of the draw with a little buckbrush cover and spotted up. I listened and fidgeted. Looked down the field and out toward the highway, miles out. Wanted to yell for your Grandpa, echo-locate him. But I didn't, and I grew pensive, and I remembered all my Sunday School lessons, and it was that, and the history of Joseph Smith and the history of the Book of Mormon, and maybe a few other books I'd read, and maybe our base human desire to feel like there is some power out there that actually listens and cares, all that swirling in my adolescent brain along with buck fever, that made me decide it was time to take action and control in my life.

I'd say a prayer about it.

I took off the rifle, set it leaned in the brush. I took off my bright orange mesh billed cap, set it on the rifle barrel, knelt in the dry rye grass. I folded my arms and closed my eyes and bowed my head and prayed to God and Allah and all the Greek Dieties to please, please, please send the deer my way.

My family needed this. I needed that buck.

I opened my eyes and stood up and reached for my cap and sure as the sacrament, the respectable buck and three does stepped out of the trees and into the open draw, steep hills on each side, me stationed seventy-five yards on the far side, behind the brush, perfectly covered and in position for a broadside kill.

My heart beat so hard I thought the deer could hear it, I felt like my hands might explode from my pulse. Gods existed! My prayers had been heard!

I got a slow sure hold on the rifle and dropped the hat off the barrel, then picked my stance and stood and set my feet and sighted in on the horned one. Safety off, open and close the bolt, live round. I had a hard time keeping my breath quiet, or slow, and the barrel waved in little circles that I kept trying to make smaller but couldn't.

I gritted my teeth and yanked the trigger.

Shot high, so high that none of the critters even blinked.

Kicked the empty and loaded again, shot.

One deer started eating, and one crapping. They weren't worried.

Shot a third, got them moving at least.

My fourth and final shot was blind into the aspen grove they disappeared into.

Not two minutes later, here came your Grandpa loping down the hill, grinning, sure I'd had to hit with that many shots. Shouting when he got close enough, what happened?

I started apologizing profusely, trying to appeal to his spiritual side. He was Bishop then, and I hoped he could appreciate the miracle that proceeded my human failure. I stammered along and told him the whole story, even specific words out of the prayer, and then the deer, and my unsteadiness.

Oh, your Grandpa was livid, having scoped that gem buck for all these days, pretty much handing it to me. I could see how he wanted to throw the rifle, fling it into the woods, but he loved that gun too dearly to do such a thing, and the barrel was scalding red hot.

The buck would never be back now. No one could get it.

Oh, how my shoulder ached from the recoil. But not worse than my ego.

"I can do it again," I said to your Grandpa. "Let's go after it! Gimme a bullet!"

"Next time," your Grandpa said, spitting mad, "Pray for a better shot!"

SUNRISE SHOVEL

A slight sky fracture; the lightest relief; a fissure somewhere above. Still dark out, but morning coming. We felt it. We kept hunting, went up the plowed highway from the Dam Road to the shared dirt road turn-off belonging to your Uncle Jordan and your Grand Uncle Brad.

Lou and your Grandpa were talking about the frail state of the world and how disappointed they were in our economic and political environment, silver-haired and matter-of-fact. These two were the same brass in the holster, the same blend of gunpowder, equally hollow-pointed.

I didn't think the dirt road would be plowed or passable, and it wasn't, but the Toyota made it up past Jordan's cellars and through the dugway and up on top of a big flat grassy piece. I'd worked farms up here way back when, too. Interesting, wild country, lots of wildlife. Now just a wind-blown snowfield, the road getting less discernible.

Lou stopped the truck to a halt, put it in neutral,

and reached down on the floor for the lever. Shoved it down and in. Engaged it. We'd been in two-wheel drive this whole time, no chains, the Idaho way. I couldn't believe it.

Lou, now all four tires with power, got some traction and momentum, and we really cruised. It looked like maybe somehow if we lost the road we'd ride on top of the snow, somehow this was going to work. Lou moved us fast uphill in the snow. But then we bounced right and bounced left and fell off the road into the dugway drainage with the driver's side. Stuck tight.

Lou kept rocking the truck and burning the tires to try and dislodge, but I knew the frame was suspended by snow. So did your Grandpa, who put on his Peruvian hat with the ear flaps.

That's what happens out here: you go as far as you can, push it, get stuck, figure it out. We all put on our gloves. Time to finally do something. We opened the doors to the snow.

Lou got in the back camper hatch and fished out two big aluminum grain scoop shovels, and he and your Grandpa went to work clearing out behind the front tires and a path to the back. I kicked behind the back tires, and used my hands and arms to move snow. Spelled your Grandpa on the shovel, took my turns, took my breaks.

Lou got back in the truck at some point, and we stood off to the back of him, and he started spinning the tires and rocking it backwards and forwards. Your Grandpa and I didn't think he was on anything, but then he caught some road-pack and came backwards fast at us, zipping by, missing us by less than a foot, miraculously leaving us unscathed and alive. We were ourselves stuck, had nowhere to go. Lou shot across the road and off the other side, stuck this time in deeper snow.

We went to work with the shovels again, your Grandpa and I, shoveling snow, like we had our whole lives. We cleared the frame. Lou gave it the gas, buzzing the tires, melting the snow into ice, packing it, thirty mph on the speedometer but not moving an inch. Spraying dirty ice. Your Grandpa wedged against the drift and the doorframe, pushing, me on the nose, straining, in motion with Lou and the truck. We shoveled, kicked, rocked, swore, and took deep icy breaths.

That was how sunlight first hit us, freeing that pretty Tacoma a second time.

I bet Lou wasted a gallon of gas spinning the tires, but that's how you get out of that bind. You pack and burn, move back and forth, use your weight, build your own road out.

The sun came up once again, though we couldn't see it. We felt it above us. We knew it was there. We opened up our coats and stood in the cold wet world and steamed. We were still out here, breathing.

SUCCEEDING TO FAIL

We traversed down again, past Jordan's cellars and shop, and then up the plowed highway slowly, traveling along Brad's seed potato farm, a farm I had a long relationship with, a farm that pumped from clear down at the bottom of the Snake River Canyon, and piped all the way up and under the highway to the clean certified seed fields. We had to keep that soil clean of any contaminants or nematodes, so we drove the edges and hiked in, or rode a disinfected dirt-bike on designated trails up and down the fields to check water and crop.

It was on this farm that I remember having the only direct talk I ever had with your Grandpa about human reproduction. We were watching a pivot water, sitting in his dusty pickup in the gutter along the highway, and he asked me, out of nowhere:

"Do you know what it means to yank your crank?"

Of course I did. I wasn't about to admit that. I said no.

He said, "Well, I guess I don't know either. Let's

keep it that way."

We never spoke about things of that nature again.

One summer, me and a hired hand stopped summer touring traffic, coming both directions, to make a corridor for a water-starved moose. The beast was so hot and dehydrated it nearly jumped off the cliff to get to the river sooner. Tourists took photos with real cameras, stuck out of hand-crank roll-down windows. Different times.

Once, up on top of the farm, your Grandpa brought me up in the pickup and toted along my first BMX bike. While he walked in to check water and diagnose a tractor issue, he told me to pedal along the edge, find the dugway, then come down to find him. Do my tricks. He disappeared, walking with a bag of tools off into the barley.

I pedaled on the dirt track to the road cut across the middle of a steep hill, a long cutbank, which was a safe way to get up and down the hill. Not safe to just go straight down; the grade was too steep. Farmers made roads across the faces of the hills in diagonals with slighter declines to move equipment safely up and down.

At the top of the cutbank road, I steeled myself and started down, and even in the soft dirt gained a substantial amount of speed. My front tire wobbled;

it scared me. Then I lost grip, got top-heavy, flipped forward, went end-over-end, and crash-landed on the dirt road with velocity, packing potato dirt into my mouth and nostrils. I limped my way down the hill, dragging the bike, chain off and handlebars bent, hiking and crying all over the farm, looking for your Grandpa. He laughed when I found him on the dirt path somewhere.

In the pickup, on the snow hunt, I retold my downhill out-of-control bike anecdote to your Grandpa and Lou.

Didn't get a laugh.

Didn't seem like your Grandpa even remembered it. Lou said nothing at all.

Your Grandpa finally replied: "Louis's story is better."

"I know," I said. "How did he ride it out? Seriously?"

We drove for five minutes, I bet, along the dangerous cliffside, and not one of us made a peep.

Really, how did Louis not crash?

We continued upward and eastward, in a full whiteout, watching the right-hand road edge for green reflective marker posts. The hall-of-fame capitalists up front had a hushed and fraught discussion about information too sensitive to disclose under any circumstances. I listened to it all.

I imagined out there in zero visibility the rest stop, the Vardis Fisher Memorial, the dirt-mound settler cemetery, the river canyon. All my life I've been surrounded by capable men, good men, church-going men, men who operated machines and wielded guns and had nonchalant and hushed conversations about big, valuable situations and opportunities.

I heard it all, saw it all, thought about it, wrote it down, kept my mouth shut. Like a good old potato farmer once told me:

You can trust me. It's the guy I tell you can't trust.

The very last time I was even on an elk hunt was fifteen years prior, age twenty-five, with your Grandpa and Cowboy Kent, at the top of the Antelope Hills. Definitive and headstrong then, I understood finally who I was in the world and how I needed to be. I agreed to go along—but refused to pack a rifle. It made zero sense to both of them, but that was at least part of the point.

I could be someone different; I could be whoever I wanted to be; I had voice and choice.

In fact, I refused to push brush with them that day. I was sick of that too. I wanted to sit in the pickup and watch and taxi as needed. Your Grandpa parked his big white pickup in the bottom of a grassy draw, and we all unloaded. He and Kent, like wolves, smelled downhill and eyed the tree-line and one went left and one went right, leaning and loping between brush, planning to pinch them in the trees below.

I climbed in the bed of the truck and took a seat on the black metal toolbox, glassed the line. Sure-shooting, and within just moments of the wolves disappearing into the trees, out popped the biggest, mangiest, rack-iest bull I'd ever seen in the hills. This rangy bull caught the glint of the pickup, or a trail that I was parked on, or smelled my surprise and fear, because it snorted and set its pace and started running right up the draw towards me, his brown hide black and filling up the vision in the binoculars.

I looked around for something to kill it with.

Instinct, I guess.

Your Grandpa had a muddy shovel back there, and a broken two by four, a two-foot pry bar with a handle. Maybe he had his Glock 40 in the console? I had no time to jump down, open up, and look. I grabbed the shovel.

That snorting, stinking beast came hoofing, panting, veering around the pickup just far enough away that I couldn't even swing. I was cocked back and ready, leaning out a bit. Felt the rank wisps of air whistling past its sharp and tall antler rack, whiffed its musk. Antlers thicker than my wrist, points all over. A trophy.

But I had no fangs. Fangless. I guess that bull knew.

Your Grandpa and Kent hiked back up a half-hour later, skunked completely, not even hearing anything.

I waited until after hunting season to tell them that story—for my own safety.

All this remembering, and suddenly dawn had fully happened, and we in the pickup passed the snowed-in entrance to the very hilltop I was remembering. I came out of the fog of memory into the snow-packed reality. No chance of that ranch repeat happening up there today—that road was impassable. I wondered who else would even remember that hunt, other than me?

We stayed on the highway knowing there would be a safe turn-around sooner or later. Traffic existed around us by then; it was Monday in America, after all. Not everyone could be out driving around hunting elk. Who would deliver the packages?

A truck here and there, workers and commuters, headed to Jackson Hole and Driggs, all living in the river valley because the mountain valleys were too expensive.

Lou suddenly pulled off the road and shouldered, put on his hazard lights, rolled down his window, and squinted into the snow. He ordered me to hand up his binoculars, so I rummaged and found them, then passed them. He sighted in and agreed with himself before he handed them back to me and told me to look. He rolled down my child-locked window.

I glassed: out in the middle of the white expanse of the dry-farm field, a black dot, sprinting, loping, stopping. Too small to be elk. But too big to be out there in an unbroken field of snow for miles. No feed anywhere.

"A fox," I said, before it truly made sense in my brain.

"No way," your Grandpa said. "Not up this high."

But I was right.

"Beautiful creatures," Lou said, "they'll eat anything to survive."

FAILING TO SUCCEED

Visibility no better, but the sun fully up, gray and depressed, we left the fox and flipped around and headed west, back from whence we'd come, in the other lane, retracing our path. We passed hunter traffic and pickups pulling snowmachine trailers and a few essential vehicles. Never did see the plows, but they were still working. I saw a low-riding Honda go by with four snowboards strapped to the top. Maybe I should be in with them? This hunt was going nowhere, and the snow was enticingly shred-able. I had the powder board that Uncle Nate gave me, the miracle board, I bet I could keep up with those youngins. Maybe. But would my ankle hold?

By the time we got back to Birch Creek Road, we found ourselves beneath the fog bank. With the fog suspended above us, we had about double the visibility on the roadway. The sun shined through one place, way up there, you could see it like a spotlight on the road.

Maybe the fox had been positive sign? New

appetite and verve?

Lou called for a ration, and I dug around in the back and found a sandwich bag full of elk jerky and three loose opal apples. These two food items, literally my two favorite food items. How did Lou know? I passed the staples up, and we all gnashed into the meat and fruit and went slow up the clear canyon road, snowy still, but more promising.

"The jerky makes me feel stronger," Lou said, "immediately more fierce. As soon as I take it in my system."

"Better every chew," I said, chawing, my eyes widening on the pure protein, the apple sugar hitting too. "These lab fruits, crisp, but not at all acidic, sweet like rock candy, tasty what modern ag can do."

I rolled down my window as we went by your Grandpa's cellars, his fuel tanks, his line of potato equipment, his trees, his old green brick farmhouse. Your Aunt Sydnee and her family were all living there at the time, in the farmhouse, just getting ready to get on the road for school down in town. The four-row Excursion was chugging in the snow, wipers on slow, warming up, four dogs walking all around the rig, marking and barking.

I tried to channel your Aunt Sydnee, the finest hunter amongst my siblings. I ate the jerky and remembered Sydnee practicing crossbow in the garage in pink and green camo. She'd brought home four big bull elk with her rifle, and one big bull with a bow and arrow. She also had six kids, an E.R. doctor husband, four cats, and sixty or so chickens. She'd just recently graduated with a degree in automotive repair, as a non-traditional returning student. She'd toured Detroit with a school team and came home with a remote job with one of the Big Three, all handled by teams in an online portal.

What would Aunt Sydnee do? I asked myself, picking jerky sinews from my molars with my long fingernails, and ate that ropey silver residue too.

I put on my gloves and rolled down my window and started looking out at the creek bed as we moved up the road, scanning for anything that looked out of place, used my eyes.

We wound up the lava canyon, alongside Birch Creek, past the pump and labor house and old dirt A-frame potato cellar. Got up and into the fog and snow cover, busting through it intermittently. The pavement turned to base, and the canyon got narrow, and the road got close to the creek.

As the fence posts and willows streamed past us, I saw animal feet and almost shouted until I realized they were sheep belonging to long-timers up here. I didn't even squeak, though my heart raced.

A dozen mutton, snow-covered and huddling in a chicken-wire pen.

Lou and your Grandpa saw them too and did nothing but crane to look up ahead and around their sides.

We passed the church farm parking lot, and their shop-yard, and kept going up the road.

We came out the narrowing and up again. A new sound, a muffled roaring came out there in the south hills, different than any pickup or snowmachine. Deep thumping. A righteous reverberation insulated with the snow.

Lou yipped and pointed and slowed down the pickup, and your Grandpa and I saw it from his fingertip out in the landscape: black and brown tuffets of hair balled on the points of the fence on the south side of the road.

Elk hide, in clumps and tufts and hairballs, in the barbed wire.

We saw the swath of elk hoof tracks in the snow through the gutters and across the road and up the draw to the north, a narrow incline filled with tall spindly sage and rock outcropping. Up at the top of the draw loomed a hundred-year-old grayed, weathered grain tower, massive and leaning. How had I been here my whole life and never seen it before, this handwrought artifact of our people here long before us?

Lou stopped the truck and we all quietly got out and looked around.

Lou had his binocs strapped to his chest, and he glassed up and down the road. The ever-present binocs, a quick accessory and appendage. He let them hang.

No elk in sight. Just the obvious sign. A light snow. A dim light. Still not ideal. That rumbling noise.

We pointed and showed each other all this without making sound. The elk had churned up some road-base too, with their hooves, in the flight. They were on the move, spooked by something big.

Finally sure we were in the clear, Lou broke.

"Whose ground is up there?" he asked your Grandpa.

"Don't worry about that," your Grandpa replied, "I'll get permission if I need permission, but I have permission anywhere we go."

Lou brought out a rifle scabbard, and from it removed a simple, black-stocked bolt-action rifle with a straightforward scope and a brown, leather-pressed strap.

A Winchester .270 from the Fifties, the Rifleman's Rifle, as famous as a Colt .45.

Lou opened the chamber slick and quiet and made sure it was empty, then handed it my way.

"How many notches?" I asked Lou. It had the lightweight plastic replacement stock for easier hike and carry.

He didn't even answer in words, just twitched his moustache and groaned. Too many to even render.

"Did you do your exercises?" Lou asked me.

"I thought we were using the sticks?" I asked back.

He made a different face, one of consternation. "Not what I asked."

I told him about Chad, and how Chad had said I needed to muscle-build for ninety days straight or suffer the rest of my life. I'd listened.

Lou walked me through procedure: if we found and had time, we would pick our place, and then, on his signal, he would set the cradle stand—a U-saddle at the top of a tall hollow tripod—and hold it at the base. Then, smoothly, I'd set the rifle in the cradle, not by the barrel but by the stock, for control, and for sound, and then I'd find the elk in the scope, and make my shot.

A new style for me in my old age. I had never

needed a prop for my gun. A lean, sure, a knee, or a fence—but a crutch? What did the virus, and the vaccines, do to me? What had I done to myself? I could not do a pushup, could not raise my arms above my head or hold my hand steady without it aching.

Lou swiftly enacted the procedure, and I fell in and saddled the rifle stock and found the view in the scope and safety-ed off. The gun was empty.

The south hillside, and out in the distance, something else new up here: cattle. This property belonged to the Church of Jesus Christ of Latter-day Saints, our church. All my life before now, this farm was what Mormons called a Welfare Farm, one that was managed by paid church employees but staffed by volunteer local congregants. All proceeds went to the Bishop's Storehouse, food stores used by the church in their local and domestic welfare program. I spent many hours of my youth gleaning wild rye on this church farm on summer nights, cleaning the dry-farm wheat. Everyone did. All the girls too.

But just this year, the Church—the single-largest owner of real estate in the United States of America—switched the property to a for-profit cattle ranch. Supplanted a grain crop to forage to cattle pasture. Drink out of Birch Creek.

This concerned your Grandpa and the rest of us, because how would a thousand head of cattle affect the flow of Birch Creek? We already had the beavers and the real estate developers to battle—now a thirsty, substantial, divine beef herd?

Your Grandpa had a priority right there to use that creek water on his potato fields. Those upstream cows would suck it all down and pee it right out into the dust, no use to us, regardless of our paper right. The Church had hired a new ranch manager too, a man I hadn't yet met but had heard plenty about. He had a tendency to stir people up. Church employees did that.

Lou told me to work the bolt and go through the motions, so I sighted in the crosshairs on the biggest fattest shaggiest cow far out on the hillside, the Lord's cow, and breathed and held. Then I pulled the trigger. Dry-fired.

Click. One in the bucket, easy.

I rolled right into my second shot, held my breath as the cow took two languid steps and nosed in the snow. Shuck, click, dropped them like flies.

I pivoted and swung myself with the silent plastic stock in the cradle, re-sighting on another of the Lord's cows, an ugly, ribby one, off to the left. Bang. Dead meat for me.

How much of this cow had my tithe been used for? The very tip of one dingleberry hair? The lousy mite in a tagged ear? Shuck, click, drop. The Lord knows my heart and hunger; my body never forgot how to shoot, even without practice; every needful thing in its season; I could still kill.

When I was done playing, I made sure the firing pin wasn't activated, put the safety on and removed the rifle from the cradle. Good, safe practice.

Lou slipped me three long, golden shells tipped with ballistic-spire Nosslers, custom filled and loaded, designed to take down elk. So Lou lauded them. I slotted them in the magazine and placed the bolt on top.

The chamber was empty, and still I treated it as loaded and live. The gun was death. The gun did not care, did not feel. No doubt I could kill. Remember the Church cows? It was a massacre.

Lou had that wild look in his eye like we needed to get trailing. He picked up his binocs but then let them hang around his neck and got in the pickup. Your Grandpa and I loaded up too. I sat in the back with the rifle across my lap, barrel in. My finger far away from the trigger, my thumb double-checking the safety. It was weightier now that it was loaded, but not live.

Lou revved the engine and shot us off the road and up the draw, right on top of the elk tracks.

"Be ready at all times!" Lou said loudly over his shoulder, "If you see an elk: shoot it—but a coyote, pass the gun to me!"

CHARGE

The Toyota churned and bumped up the draw, towards the grain tower. Lou crept up around the structure, picked the highline, and tried for a steep hill, then spun and sunk in and got stuck maybe fifteen feet up the grassy snowy hillside.

Lou put it in park and killed the engine and hushed us. He pointed up the hill. The tracks led up and over, out of sight.

I slunk out with the rifle, looked up the snow and trailed the tracks and thought to myself. Should I get the snowshoes? The bone saw? Another piece of jerky? More shells? No, instead I got nothing, just had on my rabbit fur hat and my iPhone 13 Pro Max in my vest pocket.

I took safety off and slid one shell into the chamber. Put safety back on. Three shots total still.

I looked at your Grandpa, and he had a dismayed look, like we'd already missed them. The track trail was a snow wallow, and who knew, maybe the elk were right on top of the hill? Or maybe they were ten miles away? Or in Wyoming?

We stooped and hiked it, fast and in a line. My heart pumped, but I didn't think they were there. But what did I know? I felt noisy inside. Still I led by stepping in the holes left by the elk herd, and stepping around their hot and steaming scat.

We weren't that far behind them. I could smell their heat. I nodded to Lou on my left and your Grandpa on my right as we neared the crest. They nodded back.

I took fast long steps and broke up and over and— of course, nothing. Nothing but more tracks.

We stopped.

Your Grandpa needed to catch his breath, his lungs still at sea level.

Lou walked in circles, pausing to stretch his hips.

Oh, how my heart beat in my chest, and my shoulders ached, and my ankle was touchy and itchy. Felt good, not gonna lie.

I caught my breath and stretched my hands with the weight of the rifle and stared off down the tracks, envisioning the herd, out there. Thirty, forty animals. Mostly mothers with their six-month old calves, a herd bull or two. An impressive cut out there on the snow flat. The tracks moved uphill. Behind us, though, across the road, I heard it again, the low and powerful rumble of something manmade, unnatural.

Finally, we spied it: a giant, gleaming, green articulating tractor, fifteen feet high, driven by four triangle tank-treads, each one as big as a car. The Lord's plow horse. Have I even ever contributed one scant gallon of sacred DEF? There wasn't a feed wagon dragging behind the tractor—nothing doing but driving—and we all figured whoever was operating had a rifle up there with him in the seat.

"What do you want to do?" Lou asked me, after that bummer. That tractor would have scared the heck out of the elk, looking like a war machine and costing as much as a private airplane.

"Let's go," I said, "maybe we'll get lucky and they're around somewhere."

Lou took the rifle and put the shell back in the magazine, shouldered the rifle. He took his binocs and glassed up ahead, scanning. He reported he couldn't see anything yet. Still a lot of falling snow, still a cap on the weather out ahead. Low vis.

Lou led, keeping the rifleman's rifle with him. Your Grandpa and I flanked. Felt awful, honestly, like I'd been demoted. We paced Lou. Snow kept falling ever so gently, and the Lord's tractor disappeared over a hill. We trudged on.

I realized right then that I must have on the

wrong boots, imposters, because they were not tight enough. My outer sock had slipped down and bunched around my toes like a bad sleeping bag. A specific type of torture. Nothing to do about it, either.

We had a long march ahead of us and the snow coming harder, so I started thinking about other things, like what the Shoshone wore on their feet to hunt elk in the winter. Because surely they did that, on these hills even, on years when the elk were down low. This whole region had been their hunting grounds. What would a Shoshone son do, if his moccasins blew out during the hunt? What would the Shoshone dad do, if his son had flubbed it so hard? The Shoshone were also known as the Snake Indians. Before us, this was Snake ground. The Snake did it well on foot with simple tools—and thrived with horse and rifle too. All these hills used to be seeded by thriving, fertilizing armies of bison. Never could beat back the Settlers though, our people, fair-skinned from the East and plotting, literally, sent by God to draw lines around and subdivide it all.

I imagined the Snake River somewhere below us, and the Snake River Mountains out there somewhere too. Was the river named for the people? Or the other way around?

Or was it for how the river winded and snaked?

Or for how to hunt here it was necessary, imperative, to serpentine?

The Shoshone serpentined across the Snake River Plain, all the way west to collect salmon in the Lemhi Valley, digging camas bulb and fishing trout and grouse and rabbit on the valley floor, and hunting the hills and the mountains in the fall, moose and elk and deer and bear and mountain lion and wolf. The Shoshone roamed, and the Pioneers dug in, organized, diverted, and planted. Friction because of fraction, fracture. They were here before us; but none of us were here first. Now here we were, living on the water and the dirt and the highways, wondering how it used to be, feeling bad about the cruel and constant unrighteous dominion, but alive still.

Or maybe Snake just because of all the rattlers?

I almost asked Lou if he knew, but knew better, and stayed shut up.

STALK

We trudged and stomped uphill in the snow, me following the other two, looking around or staring straight ahead at their heels. I still had no gun, stayed in your Grandpa's tracks in the elk tracks. Lou led, armed, dangerous.

We were on a great plain of snow, with whiteouts in every direction. No elk to be seen, no animals, just the rough and clear hoof trail, the tops of sage brush and wild grass poking out of the snow. I had no business being out on the flat pretending to be a wolf. I'd long ago given up the killing business. We'd never find the herd. I wouldn't pull the trigger. We'd wasted all morning driving and eating jerky. Same as every day around here. I wondered how annoyed your Grandpa was going to be. Maybe as annoyed as me? I doubted it.

"That's why they call it hunting and not getting," I said aloud as we marched. No one could hear.

"Indeed," I heard Lou whisper.

We walked on for a good twenty minutes in the

snow. Up ahead a black blip, so we slowed. The blip materialized into a few trees. Lou glassed, and stopped us.

We all halted and stood crouched in a triangle so we all could see faces and loudly whisper. The two looked serious. I did my best to match them.

Lou glassed the trees and then handed me back the weapon. What we thought were trees were just tree-tops; there was a draw below the tree-tops, and Lou thought the elk might be bedded on the far side.

I felt a surge go through my body, again with the gun.

The hunt went on, indeed.

Lou flanked left and your Grandpa flanked right and I immediately felt better.

I let them take steps ahead of me so if anything spooked it would stay in a shoot-able middle space. I worked the bolt and chambered the shell and put the safety on.

Live, locked, loaded.

They both turned and waited on me, and I gave them a nod, and we all crouched and moved quick-quiet to the highline. My eyes and hands and feet knew just what to do, even with my ankle healing, holding steady and getting ready. My heart didn't start thumping; my heart just pumped.

I saw your Grandpa get up out of his crouch. He had the angle, would be the first to see. Lou stood up, stopped. I didn't even keep going. That deflated it. Nothing, again. I stopped advancing, stood up, got the shell out and put it back in the magazine and clicked safety.

We grouped up and talked in regular voice.

Spied around the trees. Saw the churned snow of the elk herd, running east and disappearing out of sight.

We'd probably hiked a mile and a half. Nothing heroic, and nothing around but us. The elk trail in the snow remained the only thing remarkable about any of the snow-capped mountains and drifted hills and expanse, and I was losing my interest in it. The elk weren't going to stop running now. But maybe we should. Their tracks looked like they crossed a long bowl to another ridgeline, one invisible to us but known to your Grandpa. He said we were another mile across to the other side, at least.

Your Grandpa looked uncomfortable. I could see that in his face. Underequipped. He said nothing. I hoped he wasn't getting too cold in his un-insulated leather boots but how could it be any other way? My toes were annoyed but dry, at least.

"Should we call it?" I asked them both. "Head

back to the truck? Who knows when they'll stop."

"Your hunt, your say," Lou said, "but at the end of those tracks is your elk."

I looked at your Grandpa. He shrugged and made no sound.

I decided.

"Let's make tracks on tracks then."

We made our way down into the bowl, breaking through a tall cornice lip that made it feel like we were alone in the Yukon. I led with the gun, Lou next, your Grandpa in the back. Just the three of us out there freezing, compelled to move to keep the blood flowing. The elk herd narrowed in the heavy snow and cut a profound path all the way to the dirt by tightening their ranks two-wide. Like walking in a plowed snow ditch. We moved easier in the elk trench. The snow turned heavy for a spell. The scope filled up with snowflakes, which I cleared with the softest puff of breath, every minute or so, on the ready. We walked and plodded and slipped, and I had nothing to think about but looking ahead and keeping my feet.

My elk.

That kept bugging me.

Not so: my decision was based on you, your Ma, your siblings, your Grandpa, Lou. Our place, our people, our heritage, our history. This was our elk, we needed it, and all I had to do was follow tracks until our elk made itself known to me. Our human hairlessness and our country stubborness and our ability to cover long distances still gave me the advantage. Those hairy elk would get hot from running and have to stop and cool off sooner or later. Meanwhile, we could trudge on forever, never stop if we found the right pace.

Humans take life. Me, you, your Ma, your Grandpa and your Grandma, your siblings, the billions of other humans on earth: we need it all. So we chase it and take it—and we make it work for us. We stop other life so we keep living. Every year, every day, every moment, we knock the fish in the head, we bolt the cow brain, we boil the mudbug and the fertilized garden corn and the spuds, all alive. It's painful to own our actions, feed our appetites. To live with this truth in our sights requires a strong neck, good shoulders, a steady strike, deep gratitude and respect. Your Grandpa taught me: steaks have stakes.

Forty minutes passed of us snow-hiking, and finally the view started to change and we spotted the far side of the bowl, an incline of rocks and brush that funneled tight and steep. We stopped and caught breath and didn't make one other sound. I made sure

I had a shell in the chamber, safety on. We stayed in the elk path and entered the brush, moving up the incline, the three of us breaking rank and scrambling around brush and rock as the elk did, braiding around each other on different lines, no room to stick together as we moved up.

We wound and picked and I kept my finger near the trigger, my eyes ahead and to the sides, just waiting for that strange twitch. In a little flat clearing, we grouped, and breathed, and as we did, came the break we'd been waiting for.

The snow stopped falling. The sky opened up.

Finally, completely. Overhead, not one flake coming down.

The sun broke through the ridgeline, lit in detail and clarity. We had full visibility. The sky, the mountains, the hills, the valley, the river below.

Lou turned his face to the sun and opened his arms wide and smiled without opening his mouth.

Your Grandpa gave two ski-gloved thumbs up.

I shot back a silent toothy grin.

The sun warmed us, but even better, we had been walking snow-blind all these miles. Now with scope and binocs we could see—and get the drop.

I cannot tell how weird the weather has been these last few years. Mercurial and extreme. The fall was historic warm, and the fall wheat grew like in a second spring. Everything under this snow-pile was still growing as of three days ago, tall and green. The elk had been eating it. Now we had three feet of snow to start, in November no less, after hardly any for two years. Here we were, chasing elk around second-crop radish fields.

With new vision and the ridgeline path laid out, we all got serious.

The hike had worn us out, and there was a chance the elk were bushed, too, on the other side. I crept and led, no one changing that now, though I took my directions from Lou through finger signals—I was to lead slowly up the ridge and then pause at the top and get a visual before I crested.

My eyes wide, my trigger-finger ready, my heart now truly kicking, no regulation over it at all. My blood surged and boiled. Right below the ridge, a boxy cliff amphitheater appeared, a natural and beautiful phenomenon. When I was a kid, and I'd encounter some wild special feature in the face of the earth that provoked in me awe or wonder, my imagination did funny things. I wanted to bring people out to the sight to experience it with me, to knock its edges and scale its walls, I wanted them to bring their voices and musical instruments and dogs and cats and kids and hear them make all their noise echo and ricochet around the rocks.

When I realized that was impossible, I desired to render it, and spent much of my adulthood doing just that. Writing had barely kept me alive and paid the bills. But I couldn't stop, that was my work. I'd get food however I could if I could keep writing. I had mouths to feed, yours namely, and the rest of us, just like your Grandpa did, and just like Lou.

Maybe you'll have mouths to feed one day and you'll understand, and you'll work hard to feed them.

Still, you'll have to be yourself, too, and make your own pages, rows, kills.

SHOT

At the edge of the rock amphitheater before the final ascent, a steep craggy scramble, I handed off my iPhone to your Grandpa. The camera open. I didn't offer any other explanation or tell him my passcode if the screen locked. Maybe we looked enough alike that the face recognition would work? I checked safety on the rifle, then went up the rock trail to the top, as quiet and quick as I could. I edged up on top and took cover.

At a boulder at the point, I crouched and poked and waited for Lou to crest. I spied downhill toward the horizon line of the bench. We were at the highest point of the Ririe Bench hillside, a mile plus in elevation, the hills steep and rolling all the way down to the river cliffs and river valley, pristine white from the blizzard.

I panned and scanned: the snowfield, the juniper brush, the tops of some fence posts and there, finally.

Ears.

Ears like big black satellites, a foot tall off the

ground.

With the curve of the hill, I marked six sets of ears in sight just outside a juniper grove. Elk ears.

I didn't have to sign to Lou. He had the binocs up and glassed them. Lou gave a thumbs up to your Grandpa, and your Grandpa came up and found a good vantage above us where he could hang back and video.

The elk, two hundred and twenty yards below us, could not hear us because of the snow, could not smell us because of the calm air, and could not see us because of the uphill rise and bright sun. Lou and I crept down another twenty feet to repost at a visual cover between us and the elk, a perfectly round and pungent singular juniper tree. After we resituated in the new nest, we spied the elk again.

They hadn't even flinched. They had no idea. We had the drop, and now all we had to do was not blow our cover.

"Shoot off your knee?" Lou asked me in a whisper, his eyes crystal-clear. More of a challenge, for sure.

Sure, this was an easy shot, but Lou asking me this now surprised me, not part of the plan we'd practiced.

At this age, I had to be sure.

"Gimme the crutch," I answered in a whisper.

Lou stood in a crouch, spread the tripod stand, and set it in the snow. He placed a hand below the saddle, to steady it, and held it ready.

I set the rifle stock into the tripod saddle, slipped safety off. A gun crutch, sheesh. I knew your Grandpa was behind me somewhere, videoing, watching me, judging my performance.

I had insisted on this hunt—as unlikely as one as I'd ever been on—and he wanted to see what I could do. I knew that.

That, too, was why I'd asked for it.

I wanted to see what I'd do, too.

Before I looked in the scope, I stripped off my rabbit-furred hat, dropped it quietly in the snow. No distractions, not even my matted and sweaty hair, radiating heat.

I sighted in and brought the elk to focus and scrutiny. They lay placidly among the brush, bedded down, right above a dark wooded grove. Chewing. Turning. Cooling off. They were run hard and resting, steaming still too.

I watched them for a good thirty seconds, got my bearings, calmed my breathing.

Lou went to work. From a string around his neck, Lou pulled up his plastic call, and began to cow-call them, a shrill wide urgent call to get the herd to attention.

One big cow elk stood up, then the second, then three more. Five big fat ones, wearing early shiny winter coats, alerted uphill to their fabricated sound, scanning for sign.

I sniffed the air—salivated, truly. Tasted hot blood in my mouth. Dug my feet into a balanced stance, twisting the balls of my feet down into the snow to find ground. Not finding bottom, instead I banked them in snow. All the while, I watched the elk in the scope.

"Take the big one," Lou whispered.

They were all big. The biggest was broadside to me, a cow almost as tall as a bull, dark healthy hide, but I didn't like it.

That elk wasn't mine.

"Which big one?" I whispered back.

"The big one on the left."

There were all big ones in one line.

"Who's left?"

The elk stomped, shifted. Demeanor clicked. We had spooked them, maybe by our voices, maybe our scent. We both held our breath and shut up. Fidgety, the elk readied to bolt.

I breathed in through my nose, brought in cold mountain air and held it.

I had to act now.

Lou worked the cow-call again, quick. The big one put its head down and left. But Lou's urgency made the other four stall just enough, look one more time. One glanced right at me, stared. Saw us on the hill, up above. Saw my eyes in the scope.

So this was my elk. Finally. Head-on to me, a shot I did not want, not a messy neck-wound, but I trained on that elk, my elk, and as soon as that elk took that next broadside step, I squeezed off a round. Just that easy.

Step. Bang.

I didn't feel a jolt or kick, but smelled that acrid spent gunpowder. Sounded like the bullet flattened out to me. But my elk didn't fall. Nothing did. I could not understand how I could miss. But maybe I had. All the elk ran for cover in the trees.

I didn't shuck the shell, didn't reload. Spent shell stayed in. I slipped the safety on. Couldn't believe it. How?

Your Grandpa came hiking down fast. Red-faced, cleanly shorn, trying to be quiet in the feet, wheezing hard, pretty pumped.

"I think that was a hit," Lou whispered loudly to your Grandpa.

"Was it a hit?" Your Grandpa whispered. "I

couldn't hear."

"I think so," Lou whispered, and nodded affirmative.

Your Grandpa groaned. "Because if it wasn't, he could hurry and go try again."

"No, no," Lou said coolly, "We don't have the extra tag."

"I couldn't hear for sure," your Grandpa said too loudly, "and I thought I'd hear the shot at least. I didn't hear it. Are you sure it sounded like a hit? How could he miss?"

"It sounded solid," I said, annoyed. "I heard it whomp."

It better had. Really, how could I have missed? I had heard it splat, hadn't I? Or was I just lying to myself?

Lou picked up the tripod, said we better go look.

I led the line down the hill, hustling for good sign.

Really, I couldn't miss that shot. Could I? With a crutch?

Lou said from behind, "I thought placement was perfect. I think it was a hit, I really do. How did it feel in the reticle?"

I turned and looked at him. I did not know the word reticle, but inferred.

"High, if anything."

"That'll do," Lou said.

I could hear your Grandpa behind Lou, energetic and blunt. He couldn't hear us, but he was commenting, talking loudly: "Why did you wait so long? I was about ready to yell: Come on already, shoot!"

The elk beds in the snow were concave and large and peppered with long wiry elk hairs. We spied around for wet sign, and Lou spotted it, of course.

Bright spumy pink blood, red spittle spots in the snow, in a line down. Lung shot.

I slipped the safety off, getting ready in case I needed a second shot . Maybe not a clean kill. As we followed the blood sign, though, it was heavy enough that I put the safety back on.

I spotted my elk, dead, laid down at the base of a buck brush. Made me pleased and saddened, enthused and depressed. The Shoshone called the elk the wapiti; melodious, mysterious, fine.

A clean hit. I'd shot well, what a relief. A lot of blood out in the snow. The elk hadn't suffered, and I had meat to bring home to you and your Ma, enough protein to fill our bellies and build our brains for months. I'd done it, I'd bagged a big tawny fat one, wasn't I quite the man?

I waited for Lou and your Grandpa to come down

and catch up, then with them closer, we walked down to the elk. I prodded its soft haunch with the barrel of the .270, and it didn't jump or flinch. It had no more current or spirit, and was now just dead meat. Dead meat that was my responsibility. The consequence of getting what you ask for. The curse of consumption. Prayers get answered, and harvest means work.

Before we dug in, though—pictures. Proof or it didn't happen. Documentation with a time stamp recorded from unseen satellites high above the earth, tracking our every move. Marking us in the exact longitude and latitude of our pleasures, proofs, gets, guilts, and crimes.

What would Lewis and Clark think of our navigational prowess?

What would the Shoshone hunting families make of the black snake box?

Lou said, "Just fantastic placement. Perfect shot."

Sure enough, a hit right above the heart, severing a primary artery and blowing out both lungs. A precise and fatal blow. Dead meat as soon as my bullet reached it. The poor unlucky thing made it all the way here on its last breath.

I showed the shot entry to your Grandpa.

"A righteous kill," he declared.

Lou and I kicked away the bloody snow and

brushed the elk's thick hide with snow at the bullet entry. The elk still radiated heat, and jiggled as we moved and brushed it. Knowing though that rigor mortis would set in quick, Lou and I pulled the five-hundred pound animal up on all fours, staged just like we'd first seen it, bedded down in the snow with its long neck held up stately and proud.

We got on the downside of the carcass and let it roll back, propping with a knee, and your Grandpa took the picture of Lou and me and the elk. In that one, neither of us were really smiling, but we were proud. You could really see it in Lou's moustache.

Your Grandpa switched Lou out. Lou told us both to smile, but we wouldn't. We wanted to be remembered as tough and stoic. So Lou took one of us looking like true killers. Lou prodded us for a second photo with a grin, and neither of us could resist, realizing it had all worked out, so we gave our toothiest, most relaxed smiles in years. We were both so lucky and blessed to get so many chances at this.

Then, just me and my elk. Heavy in my hands.

Down below us, on the highway, two plows staggered side-by-side cleared one-half of the highway, the work traffic slowly trailing behind the wave of snow.

We had done got. We'd bagged and tagged.

After all the photos and celebrations, finally, it was time to work. I asked Lou to hand me the skinning knife, since I had forgotten to pocket mine. I'd left everything back in the pickup, including the bone saw.

Lou patted around in his coat pockets and felt inside to the inner level. He didn't have a knife either, his was in his pack in the backseat.

No knives on any of us.

Not one blade.

Your Grandpa, hearing this, snapped into action. He was a man built and trained to solve problems. Your Grandpa thrived on starting and extinguishing fires. In this case, he had a secret weapon lying in wait, your Uncle Jordan, just down the hill six miles away at his farm shop, waiting for the alarm call to come with the snowmachine and help us out. Your Grandpa got out his iPhone and told Siri to call Jordan, and the phone did as commanded and routed Jordan's voice directly into your Grandpa's earholes via his bluetooth hearing aids.

Your Grandpa talked and told my story; I could hear the pride in his voice. Made me glad to not fail in front of my brother-in-law. Your Grandpa dispatched Jordan for his snowmachines, rope, and a proper skinning knife. Lou used the onX app and texted over the pin and gps coordinates.

Now that the action and kill was done, your Grandpa looked iced-over. He shivered, and his teeth chattered. The heat was out of him.

Lou offered to build a fire, but couldn't, because he didn't have his pack. No matches either. I didn't have a lighter, I'd stopped smoking years prior.

Your Grandpa got cold quickly just like a brass empty in the snow, all spent. He needed to move. Lou agreed to pace with him, maybe even just trot back to the pickup and return with something sharp. Wouldn't take long now under bright blue clear skies, like the roof on the earth had opened up, melting our tracks slowly but surely. I watched the two friends go shoulder-to-shoulder up the hill, leaving me alone with my kill.

A wet cow. A recently pregnant mother, a new calf six months prior. This creature had spent a whole season surviving while growing another in its belly. Pushing it out, standing it up, getting it running, and keeping it fed. My elk's baby calf on its own now, no more mother's milk. My choice, my fault, my bullet. Not that it was that drastic. Sure, the calves weened early, ate grass at a month, stopped milk after three months. Orphan calves orbited in a cow herd, and the harem took care of all comers, so long as they stunk right.

But still: how would that baby elk feel when its ma didn't ever come back?

How would I feel if your Ma stood up one day and never came back?

How could I ever die, and let go of you?

I cannot fathom the thought of losing you.

Alone with the elk in the quietude, I choked up. I hollered and bellowed. Life wasn't fair, isn't fair, has never been fair, will never be fair. I had it too good, too easy, I was spoiled and silver-spooned and weak and privileged. Gun crutch LAP entitled punk poser chump. I deserved nothing, because I had always had it all anyways, even my own private guided elk hunt. I didn't even have to own a gun. Flame and steel, knife and match. The rubber boots, the reticle, the tire-treads, the phones. The shovels and packs. The radishes. The apps. The trigger, the death-tips. It was all so one-sided and unfair.

I patted the poor cow elk on the neck. Thanked it, and apologized.

Thought about your Ma, and a story from her life, back in Alabama with your oldest sibling twenty years ago. She was on her own with a little tiny kid, no man, no money to pay the electricity bill, and in her radical turn-of-the-century ethics, vegan. So she was starving. They were barely getting by eating popcorn and standing by the stove, raging against the machine and speaking hard truths to the invisible powers that be. They were skinny and hungry but righteous in their indignation, and totally justified.

At that time, your Ma wasn't speaking to your Great Grandpa Sandy, but she drove out to the country to see him one Sunday. They saw how she was suffering and alone with her baby, so they gave her the only thing they had to give her: freezer venison. She stocked up on dead meat, and a laundry basket full of garden vegetables, and homemade blackberry jam. That's what they had to eat for a while. They didn't really talk. Everyone survived.

I stood up and went further into the buck brush and then got sick again for a while. Just out of nowhere. The adrenaline hitting me still. That looked grotesque in the snow. When I was done, I took off my gloves and got out my phone and scrolled through the photos, watched the video your Grandpa had taken of the shot. He caught everything nicely. Professional-grade amateur cinematography.

From spot to shot, steady and fixed: two minutes thirty-seven seconds.

I sure took my precious time. Amazing they hadn't spooked.

I swiped through all the photos. My elk. Me and Lou and the elk. Me and your Grandpa and our elk. The elk and the landscape.

How many of our passed-on people were there in spirit? I hope both my Grandpas—your Great Grandpas—were there. I'd never met either of them, but both of them liked to hunt and fish, I'd seen the black and white photos. Hope Louis was there. Briggs too. Cameron Powers and K. Tom Porter. Hopefully both of my Grandmas—your Great Grandmas—and a few Presidents and Prophets and some Shoshone hunters too. It was an important day in history, my kill on this hill. I hope all my dead dogs and cats and pheasants attended too, in spirit, even my elk. This was a big deal to me. I would feed them all the castoff and carrion.

I selected one photo of just me and our elk, and messaged it to your Ma. She hadn't heard from me all day. It took a minute to upload and hit the satellites and send.

Soon, your Ma read and replied:

Wow, thank you, and just so you know, I'm really turned on right now

I wrote back:

That's half the reason I did it

EXTRACTION

By the time Lou wandered back alone, I was so cold my teeth hurt. Still freezing out, but no chase to give. Lou was still knifeless, hat-on and red-faced. Your Grandpa had insisted on going the trail alone. He'd find Jordan somewhere out there. He'd told Lou to come back and see what he could do with me, make sure I was okay.

I was great. Fine, really. So was Lou. We stood near the dead elk in silence.

Suddenly Lou took off his hat and cocked an ear. A snowmachine?

I took my hat off and adjusted my stance to hear better.

The faintest chainsaw sled scream on the ridges, then no sound at all.

We'd hear the scream, then see the streak. When we could anticipate the streak, we'd have our hats up and ready, and at the scream we'd wave them as high up as we could. Soon enough, we were spotted, and the sled came careening our way, stopping at the ridgeline above us.

It was Jordan, riding a brand-new sled in brand new gear. Crispy. He balanced and flipped up the visor on the black helmet and surveilled the path. Pretty steep and brushy, no doubt. Very technical down to the elk. He didn't want to come down to us, but he could see the elk.

"That is going to taste good," Jordan said, "I seeded the field it's been foraging, quality hay."

"I'll bring you some steaks," I said, "you'll taste it for yourself."

Lou chimed in, "You didn't happen to see our lone hiker, did you?"

Jordan had not, and grew fretful.

"I thought he was here with you?"

Lou scrambled up the snowbank to the sled, took the binocs, and glassed across the hills. He marked your Grandpa's orange jacket, on the move, and pointed it out to Jordan. Jordan snapped down his visor, started his sled, and rooster-tailed off for the rescue.

It all happened so fast, Lou nor I asked for the tools. Still no knife. No rope. Still nothing.

Ack, both Lou and I said, and stood ear-cocked so we could listen along for the rescue, staring across the snow, the valley, the river all at our feet, the cold slight breeze chilling our ears. We put our hats back on. Waited ten minutes.

We picked up a second sled, a lower wrap, then Jordan's whine, which came steady at us and then upon us, stopping in Jordan's tracks, our old blue lightning Polaris 700, captained by Cowboy Kent, your Grandpa holding on behind him.

Kent, heavy in his insulated shop overalls, thick flannel shirt, long goatee. Not only was he a snowmachiner, he rode Harleys too. Didn't have gloves or a coat, but had a big furry hat tucked into the front of his bibs.

From his bibs, he brought out what we'd all been waiting for: a four-inch full-tang Old Timer sharp-finger skinning knife in a well-worn and oiled leather scabbard. Named that, and shaped that way, because it is as if your index finger were a pointed knife, something to poke and bore holes, and open, and skin away, finger-stroke by finger-stroke. A literal description.

Jordan showed up six lengths behind, wrapped tight. He parked and jumped off and came down, had an old horse rope about fifteen feet long to contribute.

We were five men, then, with some tools and machines. I wondered and plotted what I'd do alone, but didn't speak up. Should we drag it backwards or forwards? Noosed or hog-tied? I'd done my work with the shot. Not my territory to boss around the experts. Let my thoughts wander, figured this was the Idahoan poem of rope I'd always wanted to tell the poet Alison Hawthorne Deming, I'd just never seen it until now, fifteen years too late.

Lou and your Grandpa talked loud. I'd worked a thousand jobs with Kent, and that's an understatement, and I'd loved and loathed him, laughed with and at him, been taught and scolded by him, and still when there was work he'd always show up. We all got through it together, as always.

My life had been work with these stout, calloused dirt-hogs, stubborn badger farmers clawing up the earth, seeding, making and solving their own problems, every year storing up, every year eating meat and taters, every year getting their elk.

Kent reached the Polaris and pulled the start cord, and the sled rattled awake. He hooked his toes in the foot-stamps and stood and revved and ripped down and around and through the junipers and then towards us and beside us and right up between two trees. Kent kept fast making laps, all of us watching, packing a trail.

"Where did he learn to ride like that?" Lou asked.

"Ashton," I said, "all they do there is hunt elk and ride sleds."

"My type of paradise," Lou said. "Maybe I'll retire there."

Kent whipped and bounced and revved, and when he passed us he'd bounce the sled to pack the snow even more. When he felt it sufficient, he cut off the sled above the elk two lengths. He got off the sled and directed us. Kent had the plan, like always, and we trusted that. But before we got started, he checked the bullet hole, and asked if I'd shot it.

"My first," I said. "You know that."

"Good for you," Kent said, and I could tell he meant it.

We lined out the rope to the bumper rail on the Polaris. Kent unsheathed his sharpfinger knife, and went down to the elk, turned its jaw over in his hand, and punctured through the skin and muscle in the empty space back between the teeth of the lower jaw. He turned around the blade a few times to bore open the hole.

Kent scabbarded the knife, and handed it to me.

I examined the knife, and handed the knife off to Lou. At least, that's how I remembered it.

Kent worked the rope-end of the lead through the jaw-hole, and pried open the elk's teeth and looped the rope out, and balanced the rope to a middle, leaving about five feet between the elk and where the sled would have to be.

"Pull it by its chin?" I asked.

"Best to work with nature here," Lou said, "go with the grain of the hair. All perfectly legal too, and within state parameters. That jawbone is very strong."

Kent didn't like that drag, too steep for him to get out with the elk and sled. We didn't connect to the sled, instead Kent cinched the knot down on the elk jaw and then tied four handles in the excess rope. We all latched on somewhere.

In heaves and grunts, three feet at a time, for twenty yards uphill, we pulled the elk past the sled and all way up the snowmachine track to the top of the ridge, pausing every now and again, but not for long, to get our breath.

At the top, Kent brought the sled, and we untied all the pull-knots. Kent doubled through the jawbone to the Polaris' seat rail, tied some final knots I'd never before seen in my life, and then got on the sled, pulled it to start, thumbed the throttle hard, and left, slow at first, then shooting rooster-tails of snow and rock, then traction.

Kent didn't let up or let go. He got up to speed,

took off, towing the elk. He and your Grandpa had all agreed on a delivery point, the tracks where we'd gotten stuck earlier that morning. At least we knew we could get there with pickups.

I wondered if Kent wouldn't just keep driving with my elk all the way to the highway and beyond, in an ultimate fraternal joke. Would I ever see it again? Taste the sweet meat? Was he still mad at me for crashing the pivot back in 2005?

Your Grandpa had dispatched Kent with instructions, and now he sent Jordan and Lou on the new snowmachine to get to the hunting rig. He also had Andrew bringing up my pickup truck from the shop to us to get bloody.

When all the machines were gone and there was no sound, your Grandpa and me, we started walking up Kent's trail, we hiked in silence and solitude, following a thick flow of blood melting the snow. Nothing else to say or talk about.

Soon enough, Kent came back empty. I thought he'd take us out one at a time. But no. He and his brothers in Ashton had a way to take out three grown men on one old sled.

Kent stood up on the tip-toes of his boots and straddled the fuel tank, his hands directly below him just reaching the handlebars. Then I took my middle position: sitting below Kent, my face exactly back-pocket level to his insulated coveralls. I was to take two big handfuls of coveralls at the hips, and bear down. Then your Grandpa loaded up behind me, standing, and holding on to Kent's shoulder overall straps, one each wrapped in a fist. Your Grandpa's frozen leather toes wedged beneath the rubber heels of my boots.

When Kent gave it the goose, we all keeled backwards, but we all held on to each other, held each other upright, and found balance. Kent got us up to speed, planing above the snow. We floated and zoomed along together, every bump smashing my face into Kent's insulated butt, then whip-lashing my skull into your Grandpa's groin. Can you imagine? We go from high to low quickly, in this life. Don't ever get too cocky. You'll get humbled really quickly.

We held on with every muscle and our fingers and toes, anticipated, leaned together, rode along weirdly for what seemed like forever, then suddenly stopped, and we dismounted on the clear open plane of snow, right back where we'd been stuck and hopeless at daybreak, but now with my pukey pickup, and my dead elk.

Me, your Grandpa, Lou, Kent, and Andrew all crowded in to hear what Jordan had to say. The new church farm manager had been waiting in his big green tractor at Lou's pickup to trespass them. The Lord's manager gave Jordan an earful: even though we were on Jordan's property at the grain tower, we had crossed a church-owned easement where Jordan didn't have permission, and neither did Lou.

When they said your Grandpa had said he had all the permissions, the manager replied that he thought President Foster still lived in the Pacific Islands, didn't believe your Grandpa was home at all. Exasperated, they all left.

Just then, your Grandpa got a call that he routed from his hearing aids to his speaker phone so we could all hear.

It was the Lord's cattle manager himself.

Surprised when your Grandpa answered, the man asked politely about the hunt that morning, and if he could hear about it from President Foster himself, for the unofficial record, that he was there in the flesh, so he could forgive his neighbor and sleep at night and not have to file an official report.

Your Grandpa told a good one on me, bragging on my righteous kill. The two men ended the call chuckling, and all again was well.

High noon, then, the sky clear and hot, the temp maybe a few degrees above freezing, the snowscape icy and lunar in the bright sun.

Your Grandpa: froze to the bone, blue in the face. I offered to put him in my F-150 with the heated seats, but he opted for Lou's old simple rig, in the driver's seat with the window down, heat on high, blowing on his hands. In this way, he'd help us with the skinning. Your Grandpa told Kent and Jordan to take off on the sleds, and for me to take Andrew down to the trailer in my pickup, then come back.

"Sure," we all said, as we always did, with your Grandpa.

"All I need is my skinning knife," Kent said. "Then I'll get out of here."

Lou looked at me, and I looked at Lou, and we both started searching our pockets and layers.

Hadn't we both handed it to each other?

Or was it really laying up there in the snow?

Lou promised Kent he'd hike in once it was summer and find the Old Timer.

Your Grandpa declared that I would replace Kent's lost knife as soon as possible, which I was happy to do, and that we needed to get moving, because it was a work day.

Kent took off, dejected, and I felt pretty low. Worst feeling in the world, to lose someone's tried and true and cherished tool.

I walked with Andrew to my pickup. I complained about feeling dumb about losing the knife, and he didn't stop me. I've lost knives in fields and haystacks, woods, and canal beds, up here in the timber and the hills and the lava flows. Falls out of the door of the pickup, gone forever, claimed by the dirt. To lose a knife is to lose a companion and work friend. To lose someone else's knife, though, that's a type of manslaughter.

Venting like this to Andrew, an Idaho kid who grew up parallel to me, but up higher in the Antelope Hills, deeper in the timber, an expert on a snowmachine and motorcycle too, I asked him if he'd take a bag of jerky as a show of gratitude.

"Absolutely not," Andrew said. "I only eat beef now. I grew up on elk. I never even ate real hamburger till I was nineteen, still ain't forgiven my parents for that."

DECONSTRUCTION

At the elk site, I found Lou around back of his pickup, the tailgate down and the camper shell lid flipped up. He was leaning, glugging from a jug. Your Grandpa was up in the cab, blowing into his hands. Just the three of us again.

I raised an eyebrow at that jug.

"Wild Rose," Lou said.

"Pass it this way then," I said.

"No, no, it's just iced tea to replenish."

"Even worse," I said, "I'll go without."

Lou capped the jug and snapped on two layers of blue surgical gloves, so I did the same. A little bit of insulation. He came out with a knife kit system that used all replaceable razor-blade refills. A sharp and handy setup. Newer technology than the sharp-finger.

I grabbed the elk by the back hooves and dragged it so the whole body was pointed downhill, and then opened them up, ready for gutting. This part really bothered me. You put the carcass on its back, and then you start at its exit, and you start opening, sawing, skinning, up the belly and to the sternum and you wrench and open that whole cavity. Really spill out the blood and guts.

Elk harvest to me was gore, ribs and esophagus, organs, sacks, all splayed out. Hearts like hearts, and lungs like lungs. Death that pervaded the farm and ranch, disease in the rows and carcasses in the corrals, all four seasons. Here we sought it out.

We did all this gutting to get to the elk heart, the delicacy of your Great Grandma, who would cook them for your Grandpa and me and serve them on homemade white bread toast.

If I ate an elk heart, I thought as a boy, would I not then have the heart of a wapiti? Wouldn't I run faster? Harder? Live more ferally? I could thunder up a hill, and creep hidden in a thicket. I had to have what the meat would give me, but didn't have the brass to do it until now. Now we had to gut this elk I'd ended, and open her up, seeing her un-beating heart, her flat lungs, her very bowels. I hated the thought. Opening up a warm body bigger, stronger, more magnificent, all because of your giant thumbs, brain, tools? For what? A jerky stash? Birthday steaks?

Lou waved me off the hooves.

"Not like that. Pay attention. I'm going to show you this one time. This is called the gutless method. The Shoshone did it this way."

Under Lou's instruction, I bunched the skin at the nape of the neck, and Lou started working the razor knife-blade in between the hide and the muscle, through the white connective viscera, the silver skin. I pinched up a corner that Lou then steadily and surely sliced through. Pulled, sliced, pulled, sliced. In this way, we de-hided a whole shoulder quarter. We moved slowly and carefully, making sure we had good grip, because we both knew enough horror stories of good hunters being less than careful skinning and hitting themselves or their partners with the skinning knife, then bleeding out themselves.

Neither of us were dummies or novices. Together Lou and I worked around the front quarter, taking the hide down to the knee, trimming out the joint. Wrenching it and twisting and slicing until we could work it free. When I could, I lifted a haunch and walked it over to my pickup bed. Maybe sixty pounds of meat on the hoof, the hairs below the knee soft and rich like bristles on a fine paintbrush. I leaned it up, snow to tail-gate, and let it steam and cool.

The elk, now meat and bones, was down to three

quarters. Lou hydrated and changed his gloves, so I did the same, and we continued on, trimming hide, cutting some stew meat and small steaks along the way, down the neck and around the weird angles. I bagged those in plastic grocery sacks I had under the seats.

Lou went on and on about how the Shoshone preferred the gutless method. Easier to keep going on foot. Take the essentials, leave the rest for the coyotes and ravens and bald eagles. Circle of life.

I didn't buy it, but said nothing. Wouldn't the Shoshone have utilized nostril to hoof, all the sinews and innards? What did I know? I'd never question Lou out loud.

Soon four quarters stood steaming at the tailgate, and Lou trimmed out the backstraps one at a time, the muscle that runs down the spine on both sides. The very best steaks. A long block of the purest protein, not one ounce of fat. A tube of the mountain itself. Four dozen steaks there, I bet, each side.

We peeled off the rest of the hide, got after the other backstrap. Muscle thicker and rounder and longer than my arm, boneless, perfectly plum colored. So much iron, no fat. I bagged the backstrap again in grocery sacks, as well as the neck meat, and all the trimmings. Lots of scrap for jerky. I threw the bloody hide way up in the bed of my pickup, to keep the hairs away from where I was going to put the meat.

Your Grandpa, a few times as we worked and disassembled the elk, would call out, "Yep, there it is: the tenderloin."

Lou, quiet in the moustache, would disagree to me nonverbally. We kept working. No one was here to correct your Grandpa. His color was returning, no longer frozen. We were just happy he was conversating.

Lou made sure I was watching, then opened up space at the top of the ribcage, enough to reach in with two hands and one knife, moving gently and with precision, and extracted a strip mass of tender muscle from the inside of the spine. The true tenderloin. So red it was black-brown, smooth and soft, rich as oil, rich as gold.

I bagged it, and we rolled the legless and hide- and muscle-less carcass over, and removed the second tenderloin. I bagged that too.

The elk was now just a head with hide, a torso core without quarters or skin, a horse-rope strung hard between a dislocated jaw. White like the landscape, and red in strips and specs. Gut-sack and all core vital organs still in place, just blown out.

Limb-less and marbled down to bone.

So finally, the elk heart. I wanted to eat that, of course, with you, on a sandwich. I wondered how Lou was going to fish the heart out.

Lou cleaned his knife with a towel, wrapping up, seeming to be done with the carcass.

"Legally," Lou said, "We can leave all of this as carrion. For buzzards and yotes. I'll keep my eye on it. Good bait station. I'll shoot them off that ridge."

"What about the heart and liver? We're not gonna harvest that?"

Your Grandpa answered from the truck window: "That gross stuff? Why?"

I said: "Your mother used to make us elk heart sandwiches with every heart you brought home."

"No way," your Grandpa said, "I don't remember it like that."

I was dumbfounded, but left it.

Your Grandpa, sufficiently thawed, got out of the pickup, rejuvenated, and got on the rope with us. The three of us tugged the carcass a hundred feet into Jordan's field and dumped it in a depression, ready for the next flight of hungry creatures, then the next, then the dirt, and the worms. It took some work, but we dislodged the rope from the jaw, my job to return it to Jordan.

Your Grandpa produced a long fixed-blade knife he'd found in Lou's pickup, and like a country dentist wedged out and popped free the two elk ivories. The remnant canine ivory teeth of the prehistoric elk, which had stubby tusks, six to eight inches long. The bugler ivories were quite a trophy unto themselves, worn and whorled like ocean pearls. I wanted to make one into ring for your Ma, and one for you into a bolo tie.

I wrapped the state tag around one haunch, and loaded the quarters in the back of the truck, the hide frozen in blood clear up by the toolbox. Loaded the bags of meat back there strategically. Shut the tailgate.

I dropped the two ivories in the cupholder of my pickup truck. My ivories. Morbid. Butterscotch pearled, a gem of the hills. My elk. I now had its teeth. It was alive this morning, running in the snow up a hill with her calf and herd, chewing, and now it was all parceled out, unmade in the back of my pickup, remnants left for the rest of nature, coyotes, foxes, raptors, corvids, worms, dirt.

You must embrace death. A sad fact. There is nothing gained in belly-aching and forsaking it— except for starvation. The sting and shock, sure, but the survival too. Humans have learned to live in death forever, the important thing is to stay out hunting in it, every day you can, every year you can, make way and give chase, and every day live your day like it is your last on the hunt, because it very well could be.

With this knowledge—rejoice.

You have lived.

There is meat again for another winter. No one died in its taking, and it was a righteous kill.

Feel selfish and rotten about it too, but also understand that the meat you are eating is life consuming life consuming life consuming life, and so you must take your place in it, and more than anything, be grateful as you chew it up. Be grateful that each bite meant one life of many lives all sacrificed for you to consume and metabolize and wonder. Be humbled that it is not yet your turn to be eaten. Give thanks even for that.

We wrapped up the rest of the harvest sight and got all the cutting tools cleaned with snow and in the pickup. Your Grandpa said they were starved, and he and Lou would be waiting in Ririe for me to buy lunch. I told them all I had to do was deliver the meat and be down.

The drive to the wild-game butcher was only two miles, but I got to reminiscing about your Great

Grandma, the true matriarch of the family, as I came slow down the hill and hit the highway and got off on the side-road.

Your Great Grandma, widow of your Great Grandpa, a man who died because of his potato farm. Lover of elk heart sandwiches and frozen chocolate Farrs bars.

Three sayings from your Great Grandma hit me, one after the other, as I drove across the dirt she used to manage, and turned over to her sons:

Pigs get fat; hogs get slaughtered

and

The farm takes care of who takes care of the farm

and also

What if the ham falls out the tree and kills the baby?

Her sure voice deep in my brain made me tear up. I considered how I'd done, how I'd tended to my family's potato rows. The wheat fields. The spring calves. The hay rows. The irrigation ditches, the flood dams, the pipes. The thistles and weeds. The rocks and clods. The ham trees. I'd been less than stellar, satisfactory minus. I deserved nothing. Now I had you, and your Ma, and your siblings. I guess that's probably why I was crying like I was too. I finally had all of you. I'd show up for that, even if I was old and not my strongest or best. I hoped I made your Great Grandma smile a crooked smile down from above, and your Great Grandpa to think about the best ivories he ever took, and why his stone was still so white. Why was it? Why?

    I dried my eyes and paid attention and followed text instructions to the wild game butcher, a contact of Kent's, and also as it turned out, related to cousins of friends through farms and church. The butcher shop was an out-shed away from the small house, both with matching siding, but had a chain hoist with a few metal hooks hanging off it, and a rail that led inside. We didn't use those though, we just leaned the quarters on the butcher's own tailgate, letting them continue to steam and cool. Shook hands, made sure we had each other's numbers, checked the tag and my hunter's license, confirmed and validated the facts. We were fast friends.

DUES

The Ririe burrito place in the old café by the gas-station laundromat used to be a Western American road-stop plate-meal diner. The Mexican couple that bought it had been in town fifteen years. It still had wooden wagon wheel chandeliers, but also now paintings of Cuauhtemoc and Malinche instead of the old paintings of cows and mountains. The whole farm crew had been eating here twice a week since they've been in business, to reciprocate. The only other places to eat would be the Maverik gas station, or the gas station with Subway, or cup-of-noodles from Family Dollar. We needed the Mexican home cooking, and all took our turns taking our breaks. No complaints from us, even if it did hit us all a little wrong from time to time.

I parked next to Lou's Toyota, empty. I got out and stripped off my vest and hat and put on a clean ballcap. Looked in the back of the truck at my bloody bounty, figured to hurry. I still had a bunch of meat and the hide back there. It was still freezing out. Your

Ma was also waiting on me—she had to give a tour at the Lodge building for a company Christmas party, and I needed to get back to the venue to shovel the sidewalks and wheelchair ramps. No one else to do that but me. No time to waste on a Monday.

Inside the restaurant, at the drilled holes in the plexiglass covid safety wall still erected between kitchen counter and public, I ordered a carne asada and fries burrito, a handheld feast that also came with sour cream, salsa, and queso, a meal that if you weren't careful could put you to sleep behind the wheel. Not today, not me, I was running on empty. I bet I could have ate two of them, had I tried.

Your Grandpa and Lou awaited me, sitting on the same side of an old dining table, already eating. I took the spot across from your Grandpa. Your Grandpa had a skirt steak with homemade corn tortillas and charro beans. Lou had a plate of green enchiladas, pork. I got up and retrieved salsa and pickled carrots. I imagined Louis sitting there with us, though I couldn't guess what he'd order. My burrito came up and I sat down and tucked right in, taking bites and pouring on hot sauce and listening to the redux of the hunt again. We talked in a round and chimed in details, and above all, were uniformly proud my elk wasn't a road kill.

Between our bites, I posed a question to both, something I would you want you to know, experienced as they were:

Why were they hunters? Why were they killers? What was it worth?

Lou spoke first. It was good to be up before the sun of the day, on foot, participating in the world. Having stakes in it. Fulfilling a critical predatory role at the top, risking in the wild, hunting, finding, getting, all a thrill, but also a duty, and the best success to a day. Bring the bounty home to his quaint house near the city park, sack up and put some meat away, eat a fresh cut, rest in the front room chair, pet a cat in a dark room. Go to bed fat, happy, safe, and alive. Do it again the next day. That was our right and privilege at the top. Nothing more beyond that in life and death. Know your role, take your place in it.

Your Grandpa agreed, no doubt, but had his own language. He called it divine obligation. Our job as stewards of the earth, as children of Heavenly Father. Ordained stewards over all the cattle and the creeping things, the fowls in the sky and the fish in the sea, ministers of order, ownership, management across the acres and hills and tributaries. It was our calling to fulfill the contract with our Heavenly Father, to manage this gift of meat and potatoes on the face of the earth.

An ambush, they turned the question on me, and asked me why I was this way. I had been appreciating their answers too much to think of that. So I didn't tell them anything at the table.

But I will tell you here: even in death, I believe a spirit energy persists, and exists, for eternity. It is what I have to believe to not lose hope, because for many years, I was hopeless, only seeing the death abounding all around, and the black empty loss that followed. Carcass after carcass, catastrophe after death-loss, wars on wars, friend after friend, the world in my backyard and the world all around always at risk of eminent destruction. So I must believe the energy is still out there swirling once it departs the body, in some format, in some function. That belief allows me to hunt. We live in stages; our current one ends abruptly. All energy persists. We are part of that, and honor it.

Having finished the burrito, I asked your Grandpa one last thing, one thing I know you would want to know.

"Tell me again, Dad, about your first big kill."

There he was, just barely twelve, up in Salmon, Idaho, on your Great Grand Uncle's Ranch. Your Grandpa was hunting with your Great Grandpa, and your Grand Uncle, and a friend. The deer were thick up there that year, and there was a two-bag limit. All the hunters were limiting out. Somehow they'd gotten all the way up to Salmon and had forgotten a rifle for your Grandpa, so he had to carry a little .22. Too small to bring down a big deer. The deer were plentiful, crawling all around them wherever they went, and some kids with buck fever killed four at a time. Your Grandpa and your Great Grandpa went up a hill, just the two of them, and came up and over, and deer abounded, so your Great Grandpa reared up and shot a big plump deer, put it right down.

The herd scattered, and your Grandpa and Great Grandpa waited, and one little deer wouldn't leave the dead one. It was the doe's fawn.

Too little for him to shoot with his .30-06 and feel good about it. That big gun would obliterate the little body. It wasn't going to leave its dead mother's side.

So your Grandpa asked your Great Grandpa if he could shoot the fawn with the .22.

Your Great Grandpa answered, "Your gun won't kill it."

Your Grandpa answered: "But what if I hit it in the head?"

Your Great Grandpa said: "If you're that good of a shot, if you can hit it in the head, that'll kill it."

Your Grandpa looked me right in the eyes as he said this next part:

"So I shot it right in the head."

Your Great Grandmother was pleased and proud with what her youngest boy bagged, made stroganoff that night when he returned, wild game her true delight.

I stood up to leave the table, but your Grandpa kept talking:

"I know what it's like to have that day when one day you have a mother and then the next day you don't. I think about that little deer. Poor thing. I think about that calf up on the hill. It sucks. It will have a hard night. It will be tough and survive. That's what we all must do. That's part of the plan too."

YOU AGAIN

Ririe to our basement apartment at the venue usually took about twelve minutes, but it was much slower in these winter conditions.

As I drove the straight but rough County Line Road, I called your Grand Uncle Brad. He answered from inside his soupy corrals, sorting calves.

I told him I owed him a bag of jerky, and thanked him for the permission and help. He was ecstatic. He praised me saying he knew I would get it, just like he knew his grandson would get his. His grandson had gotten his, days before me, at twelve years old. Had I had a gun, we would have beat him to it. Ouch.

I was driving slow enough, and there was hardly anyone out, so I steered with my knee and texted my cousin-in-law to congratulate his young son that I was happy to be part of the pack with him, good shots. My cousin-in-law thumbed it up. Never too late to show up for the family.

I didn't have time to shovel the sidewalk up to the Reception Center prep kitchen; I just grabbed meat and marched through the new snow to the back door, and unlocked and opened it. Old commercial Wolf stoves against one wall, sinks against the other, and a nice long stainless-steel table, two feet wide by ten feet long. I plopped down the backstraps, retrieved a half-dozen commercial-sized cookie sheets and as many racks and meat stands as I could, and laid them out in a line. Went back out to the truck twice, got the rest of the meat, then came back to the kitchen, and quick as I could, laid out all the cuts to breathe. We were spoiled to have that big walk-in commercial fridge, and to load all six cookie sheets full of the finest meat in the mountains, I couldn't wait to show you and your Ma. But I had to wait. I had work yet to do.

You were on my mind then, being on the property but not being able to come and pick you up and nuzzle your hairless cheek. You were eleven months old, your fuzzy red head glowing more every day. You didn't yet speak, but you had five teeth, your two front teeth and your two bottom teeth and then the next one on the bottom, halfway up. So I guess you had four-and-a-half teeth. You were hungry all the time, like every Foster man I've ever met, and an ornery cuss about it.

I always had to remind you: no fussin, no fightin.

I left the kitchen and went through the back gate and got out my favorite snow shovel and went to the pickup and drove around through the shared parking lot to the other building, the Lodge. A multi-level log cabin that had a big walk-up deck to the front doors. A lot of footage to clear.

I got into a rhythm shoveling the snow off the sidewalk and decking, thinking about the elk and thinking about you, and then for the first time of the day, realized the date. 11.28.2022. The anniversary of my first marriage. Would have been nineteen years, had we stayed together. A fact that stung me. What would that timeline look like? I'm sure in either, as a fact, I'd be shoveling snow in Idaho, something I'd always done.

Then I thought of you, and your hypothetical absence, and I refused to live with too much shame, guilt, or regret. I lived in the now and relished it. I looked at your Ma, and you, and I knew I was as lucky and blessed as I'd ever been. I finished the shoveling and started the salting, whipping it around for traction and ice-melt and muttering to myself when I looked up and—

There you were, finally. My little cub in your insulated bear suit. On your Ma's hip. She wore a big insulated purple coat, all dolled up and show-ready for the property tour. Your blue eyes blazed against the snow. Your snowsuit had bear ears, big brown and tan ones. I called you red bear. Your eyes widened when you marked me and my voice, and you squirmed to get away from your Ma and into my arms, and she rolled her eyes and handed you over, and you sat there on my hip, smug, content, cool, satisfied.

I dropped the tailgate from my key fob and walked you around and showed you the blood and the hair and the hide, frozen in the bed of the pickup. Frozen blood down the bumper. I told you to think about that hide, but as shoes, blankets, gloves. Shut the tailgate, loaded you up in your backseat car-seat facing away from me. I had the little mirror so I could see your face even still.

You, safe and secure, and still a few moments before guests arrived, so I took my chance and made four big sure steps up the front of the Lodge and took your Ma by the waist. Smooched her something sloppy, smiley, long. Took a lot to make her blush, but that did. Good thing she had more lipstick too. Always prepared that way.

I broke it off, saying you and I still had jobs, but she pulled me in and told me that she was hungry. I said we'd be right back. I knew how to drive fast and safe on slick roads.

I loaded up. You were cozy and asleep in your car seat, an instrumental version of "Wolf Like Me" on repeat, thanks to the algorithms. I opened the gate to the parking lot and let us out and got us around up on the highway, headed to Idaho Falls mostly alone, while all the outbound traffic was heavy, the workday done and the country commute flowing.

I've made that drive so many times I hardly think about it. I was listening to the song and keeping it between the lines, and of all people, your Aunt Katie called me. From Delaware, of all places. She has always been very smart and driven, a credentialed and quality occupational therapist. If not a little wacky, like us all. She and I have always gotten along, just like I have with all your aunts. It's nice to have family that calls. When my family calls, I answer. They do the same for me.

She dove right in on a question about the proper use of nongendered pronouns as requested by one of her trans clients. We talked through the scenarios, one at a time, and I answered her as best I could, and reminded her, we all contained multitudes, and the most important thing was to be kind.

We talked some more, she did at least, and right when I was in the armpit of the exit I needed, searching for a one-story brick warehouse front in the soon dark, she finally asked how my day was going, and I told her I shot an elk. She audibly gasped in surprise.

"Why the change of heart?" she asked me.

"Time, I guess," I guessed.

She accepted that, and rah-rah-ed me, and yahooed, told me to eat an elk heart sandwich in her and Great Grandma's honor, though she could never stomach the stench.

I found the building, too, right then. I scoped it out. There was a pile of frozen hides under a sign that said HIDES with a down arrow. I checked on you—still zonked—and whipped the pickup around and backed up and dropped the tailgate and emptied out the hide. All frozen in a strange shape, hard to imagine it as it was not long ago, functional and steaming. Used my haying gloves to do it, got those wet and bloody all the way through. On the pile it went with the other dozen or so elk and deer hides.

I checked on you one more time, all good, so I locked the doors and went inside. This was the glove factory. The deal was, if you brought in a hide, you got one free pair of irregular gloves.

This to me sounded unreal. A real surprise win. Your Grandpa would never buy me toy tractors like he'd buy you—he'd only buy me work gloves. I went through a lot of pairs. Just like knives, guns, flashlights, hats—I always needed another pair of gloves. There was always more work to do, and for that, I loved gloves.

Inside the warehouse, there were two long rows of wooden crates full of leather gloves, labeled by substance and size. Cow hide. Horse hide. Deer Hide. Elk hide. Buffalo. They had some stuff they didn't make either, insulated rubber for winter, flexible sewn mechanic gloves. Behind the rows of product were rows of raw hides stacked and drying like a giant library of curing skins. An eerie labyrinthine library worthy of Ander Monson's attention.

At the far end of the building, I could hear sewing machines, and work chatter in Spanish, so I went to the elk row and reviewed various and selected a pair of leather that was deep yellow gold, the inside lined with red velvet.

I knew I'd give them to your Grandpa, but I put them on anyway and left the warehouse, checked on you, then got in. Those gloves felt good on my steering wheel, wolves likes us, driving you home in the dark.

I hope you appreciate one day that you've been chauffeured by a five-star driver all your life, in this diesel F-150, from peak to peak, ridgeline to ridgeline, across the valleys, through the farms and counties, the ditches and canals and dry beds, up into the Antelope Hills. All the while you sucked your thumb, looked out the window, watched, wondered.

I knew what you were thinking.

When do I get a taste?

I'm here to tell you, you must work for it, and earn it, or it doesn't taste like anything at all.

The gloves ended up on your Grandpa's desk the next day.

SUPPERTIME

You woke up as I loaded you inside the apartment. Walked you into our warm and bright basement, long and fractured but ours for now. I unzipped you from that bear costume and let you crawl around in your soft pants and long shirt on the wood floor. Red-orange hair straight in front and wild behind. You sat on the floor for a minute, so I set the oven to heat and started washing potatoes. You started crawling around, chasing the cats. Crawling around my feet at the sink.

You never crawled on all fours, you slid around on one knee and pumped all your momentum with the other, and pulled yourself. Not favoring it with one knee, switching sides to do it, but never just crawling, always this three-clawed thing. In fact, the guys had taught me the Spanish verb for it, gateando, and that made perfect sense to me, and called you my gatito here and there too.

These spuds, new crop Idaho Burbanks, ten ounces each at least. I dried them and rubbed them with olive oil and rock salt and Cajun seasoning and threw them on a pan and in the oven, low rack. Hard to find good-looking potatoes that drought year, but I'd picked them from your Grandpa's best cellar. One of my own sayings came to me:

Search for the best because the best is always left

Your Ma came in, all smiles, having booked the tour and collected the down payment in cash. But I put a damper on that, handing you off to her quickly so I could run upstairs and prep the meat, telling her to give me five minutes to set everything up. I clomped up the stairs and got all the cookie sheets of elk meat out on the prep table. Found a whetstone and a wooden handled roast beef knife and sharpened while I waited, putting on a nice edge. Got to cutting. Stopped.

Texted your Ma, and awaited you both.

As you entered the stainless commercial kitchen, you hooted at the sound the knife was making, babbling and pointing. I started processing, cutting inch-thick steaks out of the backstraps, stacking them up, the blood dripping and stinking.

You smacked your lips, and sniffed the air, smack sniff smack sniff. Oh, then how you drooled. All four and a half teeth dripped saliva, you were so entranced by all the sensations, all your body could do was react, so you wiggled and dripped, held tight by your Ma, who you wrestled but couldn't beat.

Off of one backstrap, I cut us the last three steaks. Knowing I'd have to come back to the work, I wrapped everything back to the fridge except for our steaks and some tenderloin and scraps and bones for the dogs. I'd package and freeze the rest tomorrow.

We all went downstairs to our home kitchen, and I checked the potatoes with a steak knife. Big brown beautiful home spuds, grown within five miles of where we took the elk. They needed more cook time. I made a pan of parmesan asparagus—another thing you loved—and put it in the oven, too. Laid out all our meat on the broiler pan, seasoned it with salt and pepper and cajun and cayenne, some olive oil everywhere since there is no fat to cook out—both sides—and put that on top of everything in our chaotic fridge to chill.

You were over in the corner, banging a toy tractor against the garbage can, drooling and babling. Your Ma came sidling over, and we started dancing on the kitchen hardwood floor to a song that wasn't playing, but one we both knew.

Your Ma leaned in and whispered, "Thank you for

this bounty."

That really got me right in the eyeballs. I was looking right above the stove then, since we were in front of the oven. Framed above the stove was your Ma's Alabama-issued food stamp card. To remind us. Always. That once your Ma had only enough food to worry about eight hours at a time.

Now look at us, we had heaters in every room, and fridges upstairs and downstairs, and whole freezers full of meat, extra kitchens and basements full of provisions, more meat still coming from the butcher. Now we could eat through another winter, and another, and another. Potatoes whenever we needed, not to mention all our garden fare.

"You're welcome," I said to your Ma. "Just help me put it to good use." Gave her rump a squeeze and a soft slap.

I switched the oven from bake to broil, moved the asparagus down to the potatoes, everything cooking up nice. Changed the rack to the top notch, slid in the meat pan so the flame rail was dead center in between the two rows of steaks. For five minutes, your Ma and I dressed the table with plates and condiments, I flipped the meat, and for six minutes we rounded up you and your sissy and got everyone sitting down at the table.

When time was up and I had to pull everything out of the oven, we were all watching. You included. Your Ma even took a picture, the food a sight to behold, a real sizzling feast.

Your Sissy walked in from sophomore year at Rigby High School, ranting about a triangular drama happening in her friend group. Clearly a tirade that was cover for her questionable grades. I listened until she paused to breathe, and then suggested I say a prayer over the food, which everyone allowed me to do, even though at that time in our lives it was out of the ordinary, and me and God hadn't been talking.

A simple and precise prayer for the day, bless this mess, all of it, all of us, and thanks for being alive.

We plated up and tucked in. The game so perfect in cut and bite: medium-rare, bloody, but tasting of wild grass, clover, serviceberries. The table—your Ma's heritage table that we fell in love across—supported us all as we sawed and hacked and stabbed and chewed up all the world had to offer us, the food so good and rich and needed that not one of us could talk. We just chewed and swallowed.

My attention turned to you. You always ate your green vegetables, and sometimes ate your potatoes, but you'd never had elk. I trimmed you out a long and narrow cut, and then chunked off the end, bite-sized but enough I could hold on to it. I was worried about you getting too much and choking, something you'd done with a pork chop bite a few weeks before. Meat was new to you still.

The first piece of elk, you just inhaled. I'd cut it too small. Luckily, you survived. Your blue eyes grew big and bright.

I cut a longer piece with a little ribbon of sinew on it, for better grip. How your new teeth worked so sharply, honing off the red meat fiber by fiber.

I pulled back on the meat, but you refused. You clamped down on the sinew, full strength.

I tugged it a bit harder, just to see who I was really dealing with. You snorted. You had to, because you couldn't open your mouth to breathe. You'd let go of the meat if that happened. So you snorted at me through your nose, blue eyes locked on my green ones, me still pulling, you not relenting.

I wasn't going to let go. I knew that. You started growling at me through your teeth. Throaty and mean and serious. Cantankerous and menacing. Flexing over meat before any of your first words.

I wrenched it away finally—you need molars for tough stuff, not safe for you yet—and gave you another tender cut of meat, just what you wanted. I held the pieces between my thumb and index finger, and you pulled apart the elk fiber by fiber with your teeth. Any time I'd stop making pieces, you'd get vocal again. We all thought it was hilarious.

I tortured you a bit, just for effect, to get a rise out of everyone, giving you the meat and pulling it back, a joke not fair. Your Ma and Sissy scolded me, rightfully so.

Finally, I just fed you, eating nothing myself, satisfied wholly in watching you consume. Real joy. Then I grew sad and fearful too, terrified.

The earth, ever-changing. Time, always dwindling. Blight. Famine. Pestilence. War. Aliens and New World Order. We were always just a blink from the big exit. Life could never stay this good. Was this my last snow hunt, and you weren't there? Or would I forever be too late for yours?

So I hurried and wrote down everything as fast as I could remember, for both of us to have, in case of the worst.

I had to say it and do it.

You had to see and know.

When it came to you, I filled your plate, and did not miss.

ACKNOWLEDGMENTS

Along with the named characters in this book, the author thanks the following for their questions, feedback, encouragement, participation, and support of this project: Regan Banta, Jeremiah D Bigelow, Nate Bozung, Taylor Brorby, LeeAnne Beckham Carlson, Michelle Chapple, Samuel Dinger, Lorie Ellis, John Ellsworth, Jennifer Rice Epstein, Dustin Fontes, Ranae Hill, Brendell Larsen, Mark Lovell, David MacEwen, Joseph Mains, Scott McLaws, Justin McKinlay, Nate Meikle, Chris Mixon, Staci Nelson, Erika Nunlist, Jeff Olaveson, Tigh Rickman, Andrew Roberts, Kendall Rolfe, Lauren Rutherford, Cory Sanford, Blake Swenson, Meghan Wallace, James Waxe, Jennifer Williams, Katie Foster Williams, and Kirk Wisland

SHOP THE CATALOG
JOIN THE MAILING LIST
FOLLOW

FosterLit.com
FaceBook: Foster Literary
Instagram: foster.literary

Foster Literary

www.ingramcontent.com/pod-product-compliance
Lightning Source LLC
Jackson TN
JSHW081530291224
76120JS00002B/70